Hoping Against Hope

Hoping
Against
Hope

Confessions of a
Postmodern Pilgrim

John D. Caputo

Fortress Press
Minneapolis

HOPING AGAINST HOPE
Confessions of a Postmodern Pilgrim

Cover design: Brad Norr
Author photo: Carlos Vergara

Library of Congress Cataloging-in-Publication Data is available
Print ISBN: 978-1-4514-9915-5
eISBN: 978-1-5064-0150-8

The paper used in this publication meets the minimum requirements of American National Standard for Information Sciences — Permanence of Paper for Printed Library Materials, ANSI Z329.48-1984.

Manufactured in the U.S.A.

Contents

Foreword

Peter Rollins

I vividly remember discovering the work of John Caputo. It was a Monday morning, and I was in a Belfast bookshop, flicking through the philosophy section, with its usual mix of dry and different texts. Then, in between two large tomes, I glimpsed a slim text called *On Religion* and flipped through it.

I was instantly hooked. It was obvious that the author was an accomplished academic. The ease with which he introduced complex thinkers and weaved together difficult ideas demonstrated a lifetime of careful study. Yet this was not some detached, condescending critique of religion that I had come to expect from so many in the philosophical world. While it was in no way an apologetic text defending traditional dogma, it showed a profound sensitivity and respect for people's lived experience of faith. In addition to this, the writing possessed a rare passion and playfulness that brought to mind thinkers such as Pascal, Nietzsche, and Kierkegaard. I bought the book and finished it in one sitting.

Since that time I've read everything that Caputo has written. His work continues to nourish my soul and has been a constant guide as I pursue my own intellectual project.

Each book has rewarded me in multiple ways, but the one you are holding in your hands has given me something very special, something I thought had been lost to my younger self, for it transported me back to that intoxicating intellectual excitement I had felt all those years ago in that backstreet bookshop in Belfast.

Within these pages, the youthful wonder, religious sensitivity, and academic sophistication that caused me to fall in love with Caputo's work leap off every page—only now these features that first drew me in take on a life of their own as each is introduced as a distinct voice that speaks through the author. They are each brought to light as personalities that haunt Caputo, as friends who engage in heated late-night debate while the author tries to sleep.

There is Jackie, the little boy lost in a fearful wonder at the fact that there is something rather than nothing. There is Brother Paul, a young religious zealot, eager to renounce the temporal world for eternal rewards. Then there is the Professor, a sober academic embedded in the complex philosophical tradition.

As the work progresses, one might think that one of these voices will triumph, that the others will slowly be left on the side of the road. Yet none of them is willing to rest. Each is given space, and each has something important to say. As we listen in on their conversation, the central themes of the book—the religion of the rose, the nihilism of grace, the insistence of God— begin to shine forth.

While the themes of the book call into question an economic view of religion that asks us to do good for a good return, they don't leave us with a simple dualism. This religion of the rose doesn't abolish economy but haunts it with the gift. The eternal isn't rejected as a fantasy that stands against the temporal but is affirmed as a reality that inhabits it. The unconditional isn't seen as a promise of something that lies at the other side of the conditional but as an elusive phantom nestled deep within it.

On this journey into a faith that affirms the finite, various thinkers become conversation partners and guides. The famous analysis of our contemporary situation provided by Jean-François Leotard is used to describe our existential yoke, while mystics such as Marguerite Porete and Meister Eckhart are employed to show us how we might bear this weight joyfully.

This book sits in the tradition of Radical Theology. Yet it isn't marked by the same apocalyptic negativity that is sometimes found there. When confronting this tradition for the first time people often ask, *But will it preach?* In other words, can it inspire, uplift, and transform communities? Can it enrich lives and evoke greater care and concern for our world? This book answers as a resounding *Yes!* to the question. It shows us that not only can it preach, but it can inspire all the "amens," "hallelujahs," and hand waving that we might expect from a Pentecostal revival meeting.

Indeed the whole tone and texture of the presentation can't help but remind the theologically sensitive reader of Dietrich Bonhoeffer's "religionless Christianity," a Christianity marked by joyful affirmation of the world, forged in a prison where Bonhoeffer's life would later be taken. In the letters and papers he penned from his tiny cell, Bonhoeffer outlined a faith fully embracing the world and wrote of how one lives fully before God and with God only as one gives up on God and wholeheartedly embraces the world.

While the little Boy, the Brother, and the Professor are the main characters in this philosophical memoir, there is another figure lurking in the background, a trickster who appreciates the existential fear of Jackie, the religious desire for answers expressed by Paul, and the academic interest in order that marks the professor. This figure is also called Jackie, and he hints at a little secret: that there is no secret. None that we know of anyway. Instead of giving answers, this Jackie encourages the others to divine the contours of a smile emanating from the face of the deep and invites us to smile back. Like an adventurous child standing at the open mouth of a cave—both frightened and enticed by the unknown just over the threshold—this Jackie invites us to feel a shiver of awe and wonder at our little moment in the sun.

There are no cheap promises in this book, no snake-oil sales pitches or prosperity prayers. To read this beautiful book is to enter the chapel of a religion without why. It is to join a chorus of praise to life in all its frailty and finitude, and it is to listen in on a sermon of worldly affirmation. The point of all this profane spirituality is not to make us feel safe within the chapel walls, but rather to discover that there are no walls to this chapel.

I commend this work to you as among the most inspiring and insightful texts on the meaning of faith I have ever read.

Peter Rollins
Belfast, Northern Ireland

I love you and I am smiling at you from wherever I am.[1]
—Jackie

Off in a distant corner of the universe, unknown to the stars around it,
a little spark is ignited and a light is born.
The light grows steadily larger and stronger until finally,
in a great burst of energy, it flares up and flares out,
extinguished without a trace,
its little life and gentle smile unknown to all its neighbors.
The light burns because it burns, in all its brilliance,
and then the little star has to die
and the universe moves on.
—Fragment from *The Game of Jacks*[2]

CHAPTER ONE

Nihilism and the Smile on the Face of Matter

Jackie and Me

Ever since I was a little boy—they called me "Jackie," a name with a story to it—I would look up at the vast spread of stars at night and think quietly to myself, "No one knows we are here."[3] This suspicion was a well-kept secret, strictly between Jackie and me—and the stars, of course. I had memorized the "Baltimore

Catechism" as instructed, and I knew as well as everybody else what it said. But that did not quell my inquisitiveness. I still wondered, in the back of my mind, is there anyone out there, God or anyone at all, or is it just stars all the way out? It was a passing thought. I never brought it up with the nuns because they would have killed me or, even worse, turned me in to the pastor, an imposing priest who would have expelled me from my parish school. Then I would have had to go to public school with all the Protestant kids, who I was reasonably sure were going to hell for being heretics.

Our parish was our world. It was like being born in a little European village, with the church in the center of the neighborhood. That did not change when my world widened in high school, when I first met kids from other parishes. To this day at reunions, bald and overweight simulacra of our high school selves recognizable only by pictures taken fifty years ago still identify themselves by the parishes from which they hail. So it wasn't worth it. I was not about to bring up an occasional thought, a whimsical bit of imagination born of summer nights lying on my back looking up at the skies, just a touch of the incredulity I harbored about the story they were telling me—the nuns, the priests, my parents, and everyone I knew. I myself dismissed it as an idle thought. All that immensity was just the power of God stretched out in space and time, God showing off some of those omni-attributes for which the Catechism said he was so famous. Where else could the stars have come from anyway?

After high school, I entered the "religious life" (Catholic-speak for life in a religious order), and they started calling me "Brother Paul." I still remember a sermon given by a retreat master when I was a novice. A million, million, million years from now, his voice soaring through our little chapel and out across the eons, *you* will still be here—he meant mostly our immortal souls, of course—and everything depends on how you use this fleeting morsel of time, some three score and ten or so. (The numbers down here on Earth have since improved, at least if you're affluent; we are inching close to four score.) Jackie, Brother Paul, and I—or someone or something in what I with less assurance than ever still call "I"—believed him thoroughly, and my heart stirred with fervor. I went to the Director of Novices and asked if there could be one exception to the vow of poverty I was going to take at the end of the "canonical year and a day" of Novitiate. I wished to have a personal copy of the Retreat Master's book, which I was sure would both preserve my vocation and ensure my eternal salvation.

I needed all the help I could get with both. They told us that by entering the religious life we had "left the world" to dedicate ourselves to God. But leaving the world did not keep me safe from the stars, which still came out every night and found me hidden in my remote Novitiate setting. And with the stars just a wisp of a thought, Jackie's memory of the stars, his slight suspicion of a cosmic void, floating gently in the back of his mind. Of course, I did not dare broach such a thought to the Retreat Master, or to the Director of Novices, and I tried not to bring it up too often with Brother Paul.

I have been brooding over this thought ever since, from my childhood life in pre-Vatican II Catholicism, an altar boy and all the rest, in a Church that was about to change more in the next forty years than it had in the previous four hundred. The specter of it followed Brother Paul and accompanied me later into professional life, when they were calling me "Professor," and Jackie could safely conceal himself behind "John D." Philosophy professors, I discovered with delight, were actually paid a salary to brood over the stars, *ex professo*, as it were. (Not wanting to lose any leverage, I never told the dean with whom I negotiated my first contract that I would have done the whole thing for nothing!) It—this thought, this spooky feeling of being surrounded by some anonymous something or other—has lasted until now, which they all tell me is called old age, and maybe they're right. Now bank clerks and supermarket cashiers, in an effort to be cheery, call me "young man," which makes for a piercing confirmation of my advanced years. They are being friendly, and they mean well, but their condescending irony shocks me and burns into my skin every time I hear it. They cannot know out there that from in here nothing much has changed. In here, I am still a little boy looking up at the sweep of stars, since enabled by contemporary technology to look back from outer space at the little bluish ball called planet earth. Jackie, Brother Paul, the professor, and several other fellows I have no time to introduce have been faithful companions throughout and we have all been good friends, happy to have known one another. Jackie in particular revisits me every night, just before I fall off to sleep, or sometimes when I wake up in the middle of the night, when I just can't shut him up. I can't get mad at him; he is just a little boy, a bit scared and a bit too inquisitive for his own good, and he does not realize that these days I need my sleep.

The Inhuman

Over the course of my professorial life and the flood of books and papers and conversations in conference hotel bars, I have come upon several brilliant formulations of Jackie's musings, various versions of the same dubiousness about the same dark skies that keep me up at night and cause me to toss about in bed like a little craft in a tumultuous sea.[4] One of the more poignant expressions, which I will share with you here, is found in Jean-François Lyotard (1924–1998), a twentieth-century French philosopher. I will try not to overdo it, but you should not be surprised to find me citing French philosophers. Having come of age intellectually in the bosom of the Catholic Church, having had the good fortune to be educated by a handful of intelligent, progressive Catholic teachers in high school and professors in college, it was the intellectual culture of Continental Europe, German and French, that most spoke to our hearts, addressing what we called in those days—and the word still has a use— the *existential* questions. Those questions show up pointedly in art, religion, and philosophy, and make up the passion of my life. They search for truth existentially conceived, which Søren Kierkegaard—a lifelong hero of mine—called a truth "to live and die" for. It is not an accident that so many Catholic graduate programs in philosophy—surrounded on all sides by an Anglo-Saxon Protestant culture and a philosophical climate that had abandoned American Pragmatism and adopted a more positivistic, empiricist, and logicist approach to philosophy—went "Continental." After Vatican II, which was spearheaded by French and German theologians, Continental philosophy was the discourse of choice for most Catholic and recovering Catholic philosophers who were looking for an alternative to the austere scholasticism on which they were raised.

Lyotard was famous for giving us what would prove to be the received definition of the "postmodern condition" in a commissioned report on the state of knowledge today (in 1979). This condition, he said, is one of "incredulity"—an excellent word of which Jackie and I could make good use—about any big overarching story that tries to make the Big Point, to make sense of everything. Then, about a decade later (1987), Lyotard felt obliged to report in again, this time informing us that our condition was even worse than he first thought, even more unnerving, indeed pointless. This condition he called the "inhuman,"[5] which has a very eerie sound, and makes incredulity look like small potatoes.

Lyotard put this spooky feeling, which I knew fairly well, quite pointedly. As we speak, he says, the sun is inexorably expanding and in four or five billion years will explode. Star death the physicists call it, a thought that would have been unthinkable to the ancients. In a billion years or so the earth will be toast, burnt to a crisp by the solar expansion. Then, says Lyotard, all of the conflicts and wars of today, all of our inconclusive philosophical debates will have finally been concluded. That is a taunt aimed at the philosophers, in case you missed it. All of our hopes will be dashed, all of our fears put to rest. Everything will die with the sun, and in that sense, if we allow ourselves to look that far ahead, everything's dead already, before the fact. If to be alive now means to hope in the future—to hope that things have a point—then we are already dead. We cannot even say that humanity will be "history" because history depends upon memory, and at that future point memory and thought itself will be dead. Art, religion, philosophy, the sphere of absolute spirit (Hegel) and existential concerns (Kierkegaard), will have proven not so absolute after all. Thought will have ended and no one will be there to report the ending, neither Lyotard nor anyone else. Thought will have disappeared and that very dis-appearance will go unreported, unthought. Instead of absolute spirit, the absolutely unthought. Instead of reaching a consum-mation, a catastrophe awaits us; instead of a final conclusion, a terminal condition. Here was the suspicion I harbored on summer nights long ago coming back to haunt me, framed by a master of incredulity with a poetic flare. Jackie never imagined anything quite that dark.

Lyotard goes very far with this idea. We cannot even say that at that point things will be "dehumanized," he points out, because that would require a survivor, a human witness left behind to lament the devastation. There will be no humans around to feel dehumanized, just the posthuman or inhuman. In the inhuman situation there are no humans to pronounce the situation inhumane. Our days on earth "under the sun," as the author of Ecclesiastes says, will all have been, as Lyotard puts it, "no more than a spasmodic state of energy, an instant of estab-lished order, a smile on the surface of matter in a remote corner of the universe," a splendid poetic formulation of the anxious meditations I have been making all my life. "Vanity of vanities and all is vanity," Ecclesiastes says (Eccles. 1:2).

When I speak of the poetry of Lyotard's language, I am not criticizing him. On the contrary, it's the thing I love about the French philosophers. I think the poetry is the best, in fact, the only rigorous way to make his point. Then he adds another twist—he evidently enjoys taunting the philosophers. Even those of you who fancy yourselves skeptics and unbelievers, even you incredulous atheists: "You're really believers, you believe much too much in that smile, in the complicity of things and thought, in the purposefulness of all things."[6] That smile is just a bit of euphoria from which we should all awaken—both the skeptics and the more upbeat, both the philosophers and theologians, artists and teachers, doctors and politicians, the just or unjust, everyone under the sun, anyone who believes (*credere*) anything, who believes in anything or anyone. You will all be toast.

The prick of Lyotard's thought of death, its particularly punishing point, is that Lyotard is not talking about death-as-a-part-of-the-cycle-of-life, death as the way the torch of life is passed on to a new generation—many an institution, it is sometimes said with a wry smile, makes its best progress at funerals. This is really death, death pure and simple, the death of death-as-part-of-life. This *death of death* does not mean immortality, which is the way theologians try to blunt the point; it means there is nothing living left to die. This is not the cozy lap of nature (ecologists take note) in which we like to curl up like a cat on a cushion. This is the end of thought, pure disaster, "negation without remainder," says Lyotard, nothing cozy or comforting, nothing ecological or theological, no one there to remember when there was something rather than nothing. Just nothing. Contrary to my retreat master, a million, million, million years from now, we'll just be cinders!

That's nihilism! If that's not nihilism, nothing is!

Of course, we all have had days in which solar oblivion doesn't look so bad. But normally we get over that and life goes on. In fact, it's actually worse than Lyotard is letting on. Beyond the solar nihilism he is describing, there lies what we might call "cosmic nihilism," meaning that in virtue of the accelerating expansion of the universe, everything, the entire cosmos, not just our solar system, will have finally amounted to nothing. At the very end, there is, there will have been nothing. There is no simpler, clearer definition of nihilism than that: being expands into nothing; being becomes nothing. It is hard to imagine a harder nut for hope to crack, a higher hurdle for hope to scale. Nihilism is surely the end of hope, surely the most hopeless, the most pointless situation imaginable. Nihilism means it's all hopeless—or else nihilism means nothing at all! If we say that hope means the aspiration that the future is worth more, nihilism means it's not. In the long run, as an old joke goes, nihilism thinks we are all dead. The euphoria will fade. The brief smile on things at present will soon enough be wiped off the face of the cosmos, leaving not a trace behind.

So there was a name for my thought. This phantom thought that I have been carrying around since long before I ever heard the word is what the philosophers call "nihilism." What lies ahead for humans is the inhuman. What precedes and follows and surrounds the human is the inhuman.

Faced with the facelessness of this cosmic oblivion, what do we do now? Is there any human hope in the face of the inhuman? We have two options, Lyotard proposes.

(1) Ignore it. Invoke Epicurus's saying about death, that I have nothing to do with death. So long as I am, death is not; when death is, I am not. Epicurus was talking about the death of the individual; but what he was saying applies to solar death all the more, given that it is eons away. Be oblivious of this oblivion, on purpose. When the inhuman comes, no humans will be there to be bothered by it. The inhuman poses no threat to human euphoria. True, the thought of the deluge that will inevitably ensue will persist in the back of our mind, but way, way back, where it is really no bother. Occasionally we will be reminded of it by the philosophers—but fortunately nobody reads the

philosophers—or by one of those National Geographic specials on television. Just change the channel. Best to behave like the politicians: they know there are long-term problems out there, but right now the only thing that interests them is the current news cycle and the next election. In short, the Epicurean recommends, let's just say Lyotard was having a bad day and thank God it's Friday.

(2) The other choice is to do something about it. Attempt an escape. Take on the challenge. Try to outwit it. That would demand finding a hi-tech way to hightail it out of here, to keep thought alive in conditions beyond planet Earth, and ultimately even beyond the solar system. Seek to remove thought from its dependence upon its venerable but vulnerable biological base, maybe by uploading consciousness onto a computer and downloading it into shiny new robot bodies that could escape into outer space. Treat contemporary physics as a weather forecast and evacuate the place before the solar storm arrives.

Does Religion Offer Any Hope?

"For heaven's sake!" Jackie would have said, before his mind was corrupted by the study of philosophy, "That's what religion is for!" Answering questions like that is what priests and nuns, pastors and rabbis have spent years of formation being trained to do. This is how they earn a living! Why doesn't this man bring up religion? My Novitiate retreat master would have made mincemeat of Lyotard!

That brings us back to this postmodern "incredulity" that Lyotard describes. It's a symptom of this incredulity that he does not even mention the most famous, tried and true—unless it has been tried and found wanting?—solution of all to his problems: *religion*. It is the business of religion to offer us hope in such circumstances. To anyone with a religious faith, Lyotard seems like a man whose pipes have burst: there is water everywhere, and it never even occurs to him to call the plumber. Are not the priests and pastors precisely the plumbers of the cosmic pipes, the first ones you call at the sign of a cosmic leak? The stock in trade of religion is to offer us the hope of salvation, of something saving that keeps us safe from destruction. The priests can make sense out of anything, says the French psychoanalyst Jacques Lacan, who was raised a Catholic and is speaking to the Catholics when he says this.[7] Whether it be personal, national, terrestrial, solar, or even cosmic destruction, bring it on! Religion can handle it all. Or so it claims. O, death where is thy victory? (1 Cor. 15:55)—that is perhaps its most famous boast.

Having been called to the scene of this cosmic catastrophe, and having taken the measure of his audience, my retreat master would solemnly explain that the events the unbelieving philosopher describes are already foretold in the New Testament. This is the day of the coming of the Son of Man, when the sun will go dark, the moon will lose its light, and the stars will fall from the sky, and then the nations will be judged (Mark 13:24; Matt. 25:31). Sure now that he has the attention of his listeners, he continues. The philosopher's infidel vision is constricted to the fate of the "natural" world. But our faith teaches us—now his eyes tilt noticeably heavenwards, the choir springs to its feet, hymnbooks in hand—that we have immortal souls which have a supernatural destiny. The heavens (in the plural) may be headed for extinction but we are headed for Heaven (capitalized and in the singular!). Not the heavens, but Heaven (that's the punch line and he's pounding on his pulpit now!). At death we put off our corruptible bodies and thereafter assume incorruptible ones, in which we flit about for all eternity, safe from the assaults of the material world below, buffered from the bruises of the Big Bang, world without end, amen. Alleluia.[8] That's the choir's cue and there follows a robust rendering of "Amazing Grace," while the collection plate is passed around (with much hope).

But why does Lyotard not even bring that up? It's that "postmodern condition" thing—in the postmodern world we greet all such big stories, whether they come from the philosophers or the theologians, stories that show the ultimate point of things, with incredulity. Incredulity is just the word for Jackie's musing many summer nights ago, a nicely nuanced word whose root, from *credo, credere*, I could hear perfectly in Catholic liturgical Latin. The language spoken by God, as I was early on led to believe, Latin is the first foreign language I studied. As an altar boy, I could spit out long strings of it, spelled out in a kind of phony phonetics, *ahd day-um*, which I could not even understand. I had memorized it, recited it, sung it, and been swept up in the *mysterium tremendum* of its lush, lyrical liturgical rhythms. *Credo* was the name and the first word of the Nicene creed we recited at Mass. *Credo in unum Deum, Patrem omnipotentem, factorem cœli et terræ, visibilium omnium et invisibilium.*

A perfectly crafted word for Lyotard's purposes, from *credere* + *in*, in the privative, *I un-believe*, incredulity means to decline to believe in God, the Father Almighty, thank you very much. He does not say "I deny it," or "It can be proven false," just that it's unbelievable—the belief is not credible, and we in turn are rightly incredulous about it. Lyotard "prefers not to" believe, striking a very postmodern pose.[9] We greet these big stories (*grands récits*) with a big yawn. Lyotard treats the religious solution with such exquisite incredulity that he never so much as mentions it. That tells us something about the moribund state of religion today. By failing to include religion in his report on the inhuman, Lyotard is reporting that there is no hope to be found in religion—and therefore no hope *for* religion! That is worlds removed from the religion Jackie, Brother Paul, and I grew up with.

I now think, these many years later, and I bring this up nightly to Jackie and other auditors of my nocturnal seminars, that Lyotard has a point. The faith of my childhood and my parents' home, and of my coming of age intellectually in the world of Catholic universities—let's say the beliefs of the classical orthodoxy—have become increasingly unbelievable, even in the best of hands. I do not merely mean that they find themselves under fire today from militant atheists who attack them from the outside. That the atheists take one look at religion's violence, authoritarianism, intolerance, ignorance, and primitive superstitions (quite a list!) and wash their hands of it should come as no surprise. That attack has been around ever since the Enlightenment enjoined us to "dare to think" (*sapere aude*).[10] It comes from people who have a point. But their critique of religion suffers from the fact that they cannot quite see religion from the inside, the way Jackie and I can. They are like critics of nonrepresentational art or atonal music who just plain don't get it—and they don't appreciate the enormous force for good of what I like to call "peace and justice" religious people, like the people of the Catholic Left that I have known all my life. These people are heroic in their service to the needy of the earth and of a more loving heart than the pugnacious leftist intellectuals who want to save humanity but seem to have utter contempt

for most of the human beings they know. Although I am critical of religion below I never for one moment forget this side of
religion, the working church, which is its living heart.[11]

What is more serious is that religion is coming apart at the
seams all by itself, withering away from within. More and more
of the faithful are coming to agree with Lyotard: this faith has
become incredible and we have become incredulous. As a result,
religion is being torn up by an internal divide. On the one hand,
the conservatives, stampeded first by the naturalism of a hostile
"secular" modern world, and then by the relativism (as they see
it) of the postmodern world, are in full flight to biblical literalism or the authority of the Church. On the other hand, the
progressives are in full flight from the conservatives, from their
literalism and authoritarianism, in search of a way to live sensibly
and commodiously in a rapidly changing, postmodern, hi-tech,
multicultural world. They are incredulous; they simply do not
believe, or they attach less and less importance to believing the
old beliefs. At most, such people accept the old dogmas and the
old supernaturalism with a grain of salt and quietly conclude—
or sometimes not so quietly—that at best the old orthodoxy
has a purely metaphorical significance. By such people I do not
restrict myself to the people in the pews; I also mean the people
up front, in the pulpit doing the preaching.

The conservatives confirm that religion requires believing
fantasies. The progressives confirm that living well has little or
nothing to do with believing in religion's supernatural beings
and codified doctrines. Indeed, far from being sustained by such
beliefs, living well is actually impeded by it and too often results
in leading furiously reactionary, intolerant, exclusionary, avari-
cious, mean-spirited, science-denying and anti-modern lives.

The swiftness with which so many conservative churches align themselves with the most hateful politics, with racism, sexism, militarism, and free-market euphoria, with xenophobia and homophobia, with the very forces that oppress "one of the least of the members of my family" (Matt. 25:40), makes religion unbelievable even to the very people who struggle to believe it. The ugliness of spirit of so many religious people within religion constitutes a much more effective argument against religion than anything the new atheists can come up with from without.[12] This inner rot is a much more serious problem for religion than the drive-by shootings of religion attempted by its militant critics. It would be like the nonrepresentational artists themselves concluding that their art has all been foolishness, giving up on it and deciding to go to law school.

A Past That Was Never Present

I share Lyotard's incredulity about the classical idea of religion. Jackie, Brother Paul, and I have paid our dues to it, swayed in unison with its rhythms, and lived in its bosom, and my wife, Kathy, and I tried our hand, with uneven success, in getting our children to rock with us. Kathy and I were born and raised in the same neighborhood and we gave our children a run at Catholicism, but it did not quite take. I think that it has been given ample time to state its case over the last couple of millennia. This is not to say that I agree with Freud, who thought it was an illusion and that it was done for; religion's death has been repeatedly predicted since the middle of the nineteenth century. I agree with Lacan that the illusion is to think it is done for. On the contrary, there is no telling how long the power of illusions to soothe and seduce souls will keep it in business. Nonetheless, I do think it is bearing up less and less well under scrutiny for those who care to scrutinize it and that it is being eaten away by incredulity. The old Enlightenment motto, "Dare to think," is slowly catching up with religion, and I think religion is presently running out of steam among the dare-to-think set, which does not mean it will not continue to flourish among those who do not dare to think or read or to pause over the dark depths of a cosmic sky.

Nonetheless, I remember a past that was never present, a possibility that was never actual, traces of something that was never there, a dream, perhaps—a dream of a religion perhaps—which never existed, which is always promised, which never comes, like a messiah who never shows up. So whether for auto-biographical or philosophical reasons—how would I ever be able to separate them?—I am not quite ready to give up on the word *religion*, however many reasons religion gives me for doing so. Ill-advised though this may be, I will, accordingly, in what follows work through the memory I have of something that did not exist, of a more elemental faith and hope and love, and hence of a more elemental religion, a kind of proto-religion. The ortho-dox will rend their garments and denounce this as a completely phony religion, a poor, thin-blooded imitation of the real thing. That is one of the reasons I am tempted to abandon the word to them and let them all go up in flames together. I proceed with this proposal all the while being acutely uncomfortable with the word *religion*. I am attempting to retrieve a deeper religious atti-tude from the *homo religiosus*, from the dogmatism and super-naturalism of the "men of religion,"[13] in whose hands religion is codified, regulated, and even turned into an alibi for murder and violence. I am seeking to know what religion would look like, what form it could take, if it were wrested free from people who consider themselves authorities in matters in which we are all unlearned novices and perpetual beginners.

Imagine if religion appeared incognito, under a pseudonym, taking both the believers and the unbelievers by surprise when it finally removes its disguise? Imagine someone, for example, rewriting Augustine's *Confessions*, where all the dogmatically charged language in this magnificent story of a restless heart is transcribed into another idiom, and making it to the top of Amazon's best-seller list. How chagrinned the new atheists would be to learn the provenance of this book they bought and read and recommended to one another! Jacques Derrida, my favorite twentieth-century philosopher, has actually written something like such a book, except it is so difficult to understand that it will never top the Amazon rankings.[14] In this book he revealed that "Jacques" was a pen name and his real name was, glory be to God, "Jackie!" (I was dumbstruck by this!) This other Jackie, as I will call him, would loosen my tongue, and if I am ever dragged before the Inquisition, I will blame it all on him. Jackie made me do it, a *double entendre* they will not understand, as sometimes I do not understand it myself. My life has turned into a confusing game of Jacks.

So rather than jettisoning the word altogether, I propose instead we think again, thoroughly re-think, from the ground up, what we mean by "religion," a Christian Latin word that I embrace with unrelenting wholehearted incredulity. I will recommend here we move on to what I will call here, following Derrida, a "religion without religion" or, following the theologian Dietrich Bonhoeffer, a "religionless Christianity"[15]—once again attesting to the emancipatory power of this little word "without." I could not make it without this word; I cannot do without *without*. There may be hope in and for a religion of a different kind, one that comes through, after, against, and without religion, which would start out by keeping a wary distance from a lot of what is going on in religion right now but without relapsing into a simple antagonistic new-atheist diatribe against religion.[16] Even so, I seek to show that something significant, something irreducible, something we cannot do without, is going on *in* religion, something happening in or to religion that religion itself does not grasp and even seeks to repress, something that both religion and religion's antagonists do not allow themselves to think, to dare to think, which is what I think now. Every night I bring this up with Jackie, Brother Paul, the professor, the entire committee, whenever we have a quorum.

As for Lyotard, I want to outbid him, raise the stakes, be more Lyotardian than Lyotard, by persuading him there is a certain religion that resides *within* the very cosmic nihilism he described so well. This implies—if I can get away with saying this—that there is a kind of *theology of nihilism*. (I can already see the protesters forming a line outside my window.) I recommend neither Epicurus nor technology nor classical religion. I have no reason—let alone the mathematics—to doubt the physicists about the cosmic climax they predict. As a matter of fact, I find nothing in the cosmic death sentence they pronounce cause to give up on the world of space and time. Religion and physics now seem to me less and less opposed, more and more juxtaposed.

On the contrary! *I never lose hope in hope*, and though we are tempted, Jackie and I do not quite quit on religion, albeit on an odd and audacious religion, one that will never win ecclesiastical approval. If I am ever commissioned to negotiate with the nihilists, I will state from the start that these three—hope, the reality of the material world, and (an oddly religionless) religion—are my non-negotiables. They are the materials from which I will forge a peculiar religion revolving around what I like to call the "nihilism of grace" that the priests and nuns back in my childhood parish would judge purely heretical. If my ships sinks, I will stand by materiality, hope, and grace to the end like a loyal captain, and we will all go down together.

I hope I have made it plain that for the most part religion deserves all the incredulity by which it is presently greeted. My best guess is that in its orthodox form it will become more and more incredible with each passing day, which does not mean it will pass away. Unless there might be another religion, another way of hoping and having faith, another sense of grace and miracle, another way to pray and to practice what Kierkegaard called the works of love, without mystifying itself with supernatural forces or special revelations. If there is not another religion, then the hope religion offers is hopeless, religion is not worth saving, and Lyotard is right to ignore it.

My childhood was saturated by religion, a religion I see now was one of a loving but intimidating authoritarianism, in which "dare to think" was a veiled threat: just you dare and you'll live to regret it! (Parents, priests, and nuns practiced "corporal punishment" in those days.) This world, which was populated by good people with the best of intentions, I propose, requires a repetition, not a simple destruction. (To make a long story short, destruction is the modern critical approach to religion; repetition is the postmodern.) So my goal here is to sketch an alternative view of religion, a religion worthy of our faith, a religion without this incredible religion, a religion that makes itself worthy of what is really going on in religion. This alternate religionless religion has to do not with fantastic otherworldly interventions into human experience, as if life were a Hollywood movie or an animated cartoon, but with the inventiveness and reinventiveness that has always marked human experience. If we lack religion in the sense in which I intend it, that will mean we have given up on life. If we "lose our faith" in the sense I have in mind, our life will collapse upon itself in a heap. This alternate religion crosses over the divide between believer and unbeliever, theist and atheist, faith and reason, the religious and the secular, this world and the next. This divide has succeeded in making religion more and more incredible and making us more and more incredulous.

I am not sure the word *religion* can be or is even worth saving. Without it we would have to do without sanctuaries for the refugees of repression, without radical peace and justice workers selflessly dedicated to serving the wretched of the earth, the very religion that Pope Francis, the pope of the poor, is trying mightily to revive in the face of entrenched opposition from within Catholicism itself. Religion is an ambiguous, two-edged sword. It is supposed to be all about salvation, so maybe it can save it itself. Pastor, save thyself! At the very least it is a good strategy, a bit of a Trojan horse trick, to use an old word in a new way, in such a way that something of the old word is still discernible even as it undergoes a deep mutation and allows something unexpected to emerge. That is what I mean by repetition and what I hope to do here by reenacting the tropes of religion, or redeploying its troops, above all those that turn on grace, hope, and the future. My idea is to don the garments of a certain religion thereby luring in the pious and scandalizing my secular friends, at least long enough to take them both by surprise, which means I have lured them into hearing me out. Unlike traditional religion and its comforting stories, this religion will not ensure that we will all get more sleep. On the contrary, it ensures an endless conversation with the specters of the night.

Itinerary

For such an ambitious undertaking, I require help. This I find throughout in the mystics, figures who first paid a visit to Brother Paul and made a lasting impression upon an impressionable young man. In this book, the mystics play a special role as the insiders in religion, whose bold strokes cut to the core of religion, while all along being outsiders who unnerve the powers-that-be on the inside. The structure of this slash, of this inside/outside, within/without (another postmodern trope), is crucial to the line I am advancing here, where the trick is not to let one side get the better of the other. I will first explain my lifelong taste for the mystics (chapter 2). They sound the depths of our everyday and quotidian lives and have helped pave the way for the modern and postmodern world we live in. I will then turn to two familiar, everyday, commonplace experiences—giving a gift and hospitality—and propose that each of them trembles with mystical depth and each represents a powerful and important ingredient in the case I am making for a postmodern religion (chapters 3–5). That is all by way of amassing evidence to present to the court for the position I take on God, about whom I will say a few things that would have scared Jackie and Brother

Paul half to death (chapter 6). After a brief interlude in which Jackie and Brother Paul express their misgivings to the professor's ways, I formulate a repetition of religion, a religion without religion, which turns on what I call the *nihilism of grace*, all of which would definitely have gotten me expelled from my parish school (chapters 7–9). That will explain why Jackie, Brother Paul, the professor, and I have spent our entire life together praying like hell (chapter 10).

The rose is without why; it blossoms because it blossoms;
It cares not for itself, asks not if it's seen.
—Angelus Silesius

CHAPTER TWO

A Taste for
the Mystics

I spent a certain amount of time in a thirteenth-century mon-
astery. To be honest, we did have electricity, indoor plumb-
ing, and central heating (but no air conditioning). Otherwise
nothing much had changed. We followed an ancient timetable,
roused from our sleep by a large loud bell at 5:00 a.m. for a
couple hours of prayer, meditation, and Mass before breakfast—
to "break" a "fast" was just a word to me before that time. That
was followed by a day of *ora et labora*, manual labor, study, and

more prayer, meals taken in silence while listening to a "spiritual reading," chanting the psalms in Latin and English on alternate days. Then to bed and the "great silence," and it all started over again the next morning. The period of formation in the Novitiate lasted fifteen months, three months of postulancy (asking to be admitted) and a canonical year and a day as a novice, culminating in first vows. Fortunately, we were only eighteen years old, and we were ideal recruits for a religious bootcamp, willing to do what we were told.

The order was French and it called the Novitiate a *normal* school, a term seized upon by Michel Foucault, who as I discovered years later skewered our founder for introducing "normalizing" practices into French education.[1] The following three years, the scholasticate, when we were sent to the university, were quite different and proved to be a very exciting time for me—exciting in an interior sort of way, I hasten to add, as we were still in formation. I was a frat boy but the frat was the *Fratres Scholarum Christianarum* (F.S.C., Brothers of the Christian Schools). It was then, the time of Brother Paul, that I was introduced both to the mystics and to the metaphysics of Thomas Aquinas. The mix of mysticism and metaphysics, and the task of exploring the borders between faith and philosophy, has filled my head ever since. I acquired a lifelong taste for the mystics, for these extravagant disturbers of the ecclesiastical peace, whose own taste for the audacious has often bought them a considerable amount of trouble.

The Rose Is without Why

After four years, I left the religious life. The De LaSalle Brothers were for the most part high school teachers and I was being prepared to teach high school English and Religion. But in the course of my undergraduate studies I had been exposed to quite a lot of philosophy and it had struck like lightning. So at the end of the fourth of five years of formation I presented myself to Brother Provincial, the man who ran the Middle Atlantic states province of Brothers to which I belonged, and I stated my case. At the end of the years of formation, I wanted to go to Fordham University, a Jesuit university that in addition to its classical Catholic curriculum included a focus on Continental philosophy, to take my Ph.D. in philosophy and come back to teach philosophy at LaSalle University (then still a college) in Philadelphia. I promised him I would be good at it. His response was that I had taken a vow of obedience and that all that should matter to me was the "will of God as it is expressed for me by the will of my superiors," a phrase I had heard many times before. What I wanted might someday happen, he said, unless it did not! But I might well spend the rest of my life working in the orphanage the Brothers ran. It should not matter to me, he said.

But matter it did. This was pre-Vatican II, Council of Trent Catholicism. As Thomas Merton pointed out, it's funny how in those days the will of God could come down to the will of an Italian undersecretary in the Holy Office.[2] A year later, when Pope John XXIII convened one of the most important Councils in the history of the Church, everything would change. Only then would it dawn upon the religious orders that their idea of the will of God ought to be expanded to include the God-given talents of their members if they hoped to survive in the modern world. We would all be excited by Vatican II, the way we are all excited today by Pope Francis even as we hope that his work will not be undone by his successors, as happened to John

XXIII. But neither Brother Provincial nor Brother Paul had ever heard of Vatican II. So I thanked him for the many gifts I had been given in my four precious years as a Brother, one of which was to have discovered my vocation—the life of a philosopher— for which I have been grateful all my life.

But I soon learned there was to be no clear line of separation between religion and my philosophical life. Every time I thought I had left religion behind, I found it waiting for me around the next corner, its arms crossed, with a grin on its face, as if to say, "it's about time you showed up." In graduate school, my interest in existentialism and phenomenology, whose stock was sky high in those days, drew me quickly to Heidegger's *Being and Time*, the bible of that movement and a book of elemental importance for me, for my generation, and for twentieth-century Continental philosophy at large. I was drawn to Heidegger in particular not only because he was the most eminent Continental philosopher of the day but also because of his provenance in a conservative Catholicism and his familiarity with the medieval philosophers and mystics. There was a time when he was a young man that Heidegger was thought to be the rising star of German Catholic philosophy. But it was the "later" Heidegger who would eventually command my attention. My first serious work as a scholar was a study of Heidegger and Meister Eckhart, the greatest of the Rhineland mystics.[3] As soon as I began reading the works Heidegger published after World War II—most of the younger generation of Americans in those days, who grew up after the end of the war, knew next to nothing then about the "Heidegger Affair" (his entanglement with the Nazis)—I immediately recognized the echoes of the mystics, the constant companions of me and Brother Paul for four years.

At the end of his career, Heidegger gave a brilliant series of lectures under the title *The Principle of Reason* (1955–56), of which the centerpiece was a verse from *The Cherubinic Wanderer*, a poem by Angelus Silesius—the "Silesian Angel," a pen name employed by Johannes Scheffler (1624–77). Heidegger juxtaposed the philosophical principle of sufficient reason—"nothing is without reason"—with this verse:

> The rose is without why; it blossoms because it
>   blossoms;
> It cares not for itself, asks not if it's seen.[4]

Challenging both common sense and sophisticated logic alike, which tell us that everything has a reason, the mystical poet paradoxically says the rose does not have a reason.

The glory of the rose is the glory of living without why, untroubled by all the why's and wherefore's of the philosophers and theologians that beset their restless minds. The poetic verse does not put these questions to rest by answering them so much as it cuts them off before they get started. It does not solve the problems posed by the philosophers and theologians so much as it dissolves them, putting them out of play before they get on the field. The poet invites us to enter a space where these questions never come up in the first place, a space where asking why is out of place, where everyone in earshot would be shocked by such an impertinent breach of protocol. Instead of subjecting the being of the rose to cross-examination, we are counseled by the mystical poet to bask in the being-a-rose of the rose, to revel in its rose-hood. To slightly adapt what Archibald MacLeish said in the last line of his famous poem about the poem, the rose "should not mean / But be."[5]

This is all well and good, and we all grant poets the license to say very poetic things, but things quickly get more complicated when the prose of the world makes its presence felt. For one thing, is not the mystical poet simply pointing out the obvious: that the rose is not like us human beings, we who think and worry, who search and question all the time? To be sure. But while that is true on the prosaic level, the poet is suggesting that there is another sphere below the surface where things happen without all that worrying, before such questions and concerns arrive at the scene. As Heidegger said, the poet's point is not that the rose is unlike us, but exactly the opposite, that we should take the rose as our model, that in the deepest part of our being we should be like the rose. We too should live "without why," allowing life to blossom without weighing it down with our why's and wherefore's.[6] (Otherwise the biblical-poetic saying about living like the lilies of the field would have no purchase on our lives.) But that cannot be the whole answer. For we neither can nor should stop asking why, lest we be victimized by all the outrages of authoritarianism and blind obedience, of superstition and unthinking prejudice. Every advance made in human affairs has depended upon people who look upon how things are and ask why they cannot be otherwise. After all, we owe the Enlightenment too much to simply show it the door, on the word of a single pseudonymous Silesian poet.

But notice, Heidegger points out, the poet is not saying that the rose is without grounds—it blossoms *because* it blossoms—but that it is without why. He is not denying that the rose has a cause or a because, a complex set of causes and conditions that are known to every gardener and investigated in detail by the botanist. Instead the poet is insisting upon a still deeper, prior, or different sphere, where the search for grounds, for causes and effects, is suspended, where all of our why's are put out of play. We are invited to repose in the rose, to allow the rose to rise up and *be* a rose—where the philosopher (Heidegger) and the poet (MacLeish) are using "be" in a tantalizingly similar way. The rose is a poetic thing, and as such meant to stand for *every*thing, *tout le monde*, the French say, the whole world! This thing and that thing have causes and reasons and we can and should and must seek out their why's and their wherefore's. But the poetic role is to reveal another land or region, so that the sphere of asking why does not swallow us whole. Here the very "being" there at all of the rose, of anything at all, ourselves, the starry heavens above and the moral law within, the very being there at all of the world, all this why-and-wherefore-ing runs up against its limit or rather never gets off the ground.

There we find ourselves face-to-face with something "lovely, dark and deep," as Robert Frost famously said, forced to pause over something simple and mysterious, which fills us with wonder, whose simple being-there is best savored and not interrogated, best left to *be*. We catch sight of the glory (*doxa*) of the rose, the glory of the world, which means that Angelus Silesius' poem is a kind of doxology,[7] a song of praise to the world in the figure of the blossoming of the rose. Glory be to the rose, glory be to dappled things. By checking our interrogatory frame of mind at the door, we let the rose be a rose. Such *letting be*, we hasten to add, is nothing negative, not a matter of indifference, and it does not just happen, as if on automatic pilot. To let the rose be a rose we must *do* something, learn to practice a rigorous discipline, an asceticism, a hard-won simplicity and detachment, as all the mystical masters, East and West, can confirm. We must learn how to live like the rose, without why, by withdrawing the rose from the system of means and ends, where it serves some ultimate end or purpose, all of which dims the glory of the rose.

When I first came across all this as a graduate student, working on my dissertation, and then pursuing it further as a young professor working on my first book, I recognized everything they were telling us in the Novitiate, the whole constellation of detachment, nothingness, and letting God be God in everything we said or did. The memories of Brother Paul came flooding back upon me, the 5:00 a.m. rising bell, the psalms, the long hours of prayer and meditation. I knew that what I was looking for was to be found there, somewhere, perhaps—as I would eventually conclude—in some underground space beneath my "religious life" and my professorial-philosophical life. I began publishing with a fury about these matters, in part to get tenure and promotion; there was no denying that. The economic world is always there; it is not a question of leaving it behind but of not allowing it a stranglehold. But I was also writing about these things because they were the passion of my life, because I was searching for Kierkegaard's truth to live and die for—and they were actually paying me to do so! I never, ever told the administration I would have done the whole thing for nothing! In fact, whenever they saw me coming they thought I was there to demand a raise. Doing things for nothing, while still earning a living wage—what is that if not the meaning of life? That was the beginning of what I am calling here the nihilism of grace.

Needless to say, Jackie visited me every night to see what progress we were making.

The Conditional and the Unconditional

Consequently, I have invested all my funds in this little mystical verse and the massive mystical tradition upon which it is drawing. I treat the mystical word as a word to the wise that will be central to the case I want to make for thinking about religion otherwise. I accept everything the mystics say, except for the one thing I don't accept.

The classical Christian mystics tend to cast this distinction in dualist terms. They make the distinction between living with and without a why into a distinction between time and eternity, between the body and the soul. They oppose the busy buzzing flow of the sensible world to the eternal peace of the super-sensible world. This bipolarity has dominated classical theology, including mystical theology, and that, as I slowly began to realize, was becoming completely unbelievable to me. I think Jackie wondered just a bit about it, and I even think Brother Paul did, too, although he did not quite admit it either to himself or his superiors. But the older I got, the less the professor and I believed it. I am retired now and the string of years I will have been granted is running out. Now more than ever it would be comforting to think that death is a doorway to eternal life. But as death becomes more real, I greet eternity with increasing incredulity. This dualism seems to me to have been induced in the mystics by a bit of an overdose on Greek philosophy in which time is mistreated as an imperfect imitation of eternity, as a moving image of something immovable. So the great mystics of the "without why"—Meister Eckhart, my hero, among them—regard living "without why" as a foretaste and anticipation of eternal life that we are granted while we still live here below, as an island of eternal peace right now while the turbulent waters of time still swirl all around.

There I dare to differ. I think they have gotten the *experience* right. There are things we simply savor and appreciate and do not interrogate, whose worth we simply affirm but do not feel obliged to justify. This is the sort of thing of which we say, "You can't put a price on that." But they have overloaded this experience and almost sunk it with the heavy baggage of a bipolar Greek philosophy, its *metaphysics*, meaning the "physical—and beyond." The real distinction is not between time and eternity but between two different kinds of time. The first is the time of planning and calculating and worrying about how to make ends meet—which no one can dismiss. Having since gotten married, I quickly realized that we need to plan for our future, for our children's future, and for all the needs and necessities of life. We have to pay the mortgage—which is why my instincts told me not to tell the dean that he didn't have to pay me. Let us call that the time of the *conditional*, of doing this for the sake of that, doing this as a condition for achieving that, the way we brush our teeth in order to avoid cavities. The other is the time of the "*unconditional.*" These are the times when something comes over us that is savored for itself. Then we find ourselves doing things that we are not doing *for* something else but for themselves, unconditionally.

Robert Frost got this right, not the Neoplatonist theologians. His poetic meditation upon the snowy woods comes as a "pause" in the flow of time, after which the rider must move on: "but I have promises to keep and miles to go before I sleep." Living without why has nothing to do with the timelessness of eternity but with the exquisite timeliness of the precisely timed pause, of the moment when time is suspended, of the interruption of a temporal flow, which are often the most significant moments of all. In the time of the unconditional, something is affirmed for itself, without why. The unconditional is found not in eternity but in a caesura inside time; it is made entirely of time; it is time all the way down. Think of a pause in the middle of a piece of music which is entirely shaped by the melody that precedes and follows it, or of a pregnant pause in language, a moment of silence which is entirely shaped by what was just said and what is about to be said next.

These are moments when the demands of daily life, the stream of conditions and calculations in which we are immersed—the promises we have to keep—are suspended. Then we live in the moment of something incalculable, behaving as if we had all the time in the world. Such moments in time do not provide off-ramps into eternity. Such experiences do not signal another world but embody another way of being in this world. In them we catch a glimpse not of eternal life but of living otherwise in this life. They are not intimations of immortality but, on the contrary, forcible reminders of mortality that make us prize this fleeting moment all the more. They intensify the moment to the limit.

The way the professor and I would put this now follows the lead of the other Jackie (Derrida), my favorite of the "Sixty-Eighters," the generation of French thinkers who came after Heidegger and stole the thunder of genuinely original philosophy from the Germans, making Paris the magnetic center of Continental philosophy. I too was something of a Sixty-Eighter, all by myself. That is the year—the year whose political upheavals rocked both France and the United States—that Kathy and I were married, I finished my doctoral studies, and assumed a teaching position in the philosophy department at Villanova University. I taught at Villanova for thirty-six years before I took early retirement in order to spend seven years in the religion department at Syracuse. So what I would say now is that these mystics have hit upon the deepest of distinctions, not between time and eternity, but between the *time of an economy* and the *time of the gift*. In economic life, everything has a why and every investment is expected to have a return. But the gift is given without regard to such considerations; the gift is given with nothing up our sleeve, unconditionally, without why. We may not even be able to afford the gift we give, like the widow who gave of her very substance (Luke 21:4), and we are not looking ahead for future dividends.

So instead of distinguishing between time and eternity, body and soul, mortality and immortality—in which my beloved mystics let their Greco-philosophical imaginations run wild—let us say instead there is something *conditional* about the rose and also something *unconditional*.

On the one hand, the rose depends upon and is subject to a series of biological conditions without which it would not exist at all. There would be no rose were it not for the soil, sun, and moisture by which it is nourished, the conditions and causes that only careful scientific inquiry can explain, all of which has a majesty of its own. One of the more serious mistakes I made as a young philosopher was to put all my chips on philosophy, religion, and art and to have underestimated the wonders that the scientists were disclosing, especially about the stars! In that sense, nothing is without a reason. Without the Principle of Reason, we would still think the earth is flat and at the center of the universe; without it, there is nothing to protect children from being taught that Adam and Eve are historical persons created by a special act of God with no relation to previous forms of life; without it, there is nothing to protect religion from becoming the laughingstock it makes itself to people who pause to think about things; without it there is nothing to protect us from the violence of religion, which of course is when religion is no laughing matter.

But on the other hand, there is also something unconditional about the rose, its glory, its unconditional splendor, its sheer effulgence, and that is what the mystical poet has in view. That is why we pause over snowy woods or the blossoming of the rose—or an old watch that has not worked in years but was given to us at our graduation by our parents now long dead, things of incalculable worth. The list is endless, and it is not a list of different *things* but of two different ways of *regarding* things. *Anything* can take on this incandescence given the right circumstances. Given the right *conditions* anything can rise up or break out into *un*conditional splendor or unconditional worth. The unconditional is embedded deeply in the most quotidian things, things as simple as the rose. At such moments the task is to let the rose *be* the rose that it is, not in the sense of causing it to be, bringing it into existence—so I am linking existence with real causes and conditions on the ground—but in the sense of savoring its splendor, immersing ourselves in its majesty, its sheer givenness or—here is my term of choice—its sheer *grace*. The caesura is a moment of grace and hence a religious moment for me, because the religion I am trying to retrieve in the present text begins and ends with grace. *Where there is grace, there is religion; where there is religion, there is grace.* We let the rose interrupt the rush of existence, stop us in our tracks, bring us up short. We let it speak to us of the mystery of our very being in the world at all, of there being any world at all, of something whose worth we prize unconditionally. In that sense, "The rose is without why."

It should be clear from what I am saying that it would never be a matter of choosing between the conditional and the unconditional. The two belong together, like up and down, inside and outside. Otherwise theology will be seduced into the bipolarism and dualism of time and eternity. The history of theology from Philo of Alexandria (c. 20 BCE–c. 50 CE) to the present is the history of varying degrees and shades of dualism, sometimes extreme, sometime mitigated, but always of two worlds: one here in space and time and another—well, God knows where! Without the string of conditions, the rose would not exist at all in the sense of its actuality or factual reality. To ignore the conditions of actuality or reality would turn the magic in life into believing in magic pure and simple; it would confuse poetry with illusion, and grace with superstition, which is what I am constantly criticizing and what I hold responsible for the incredulity that religion has earned for itself.

But without the mystical poet's sense of the unconditional, everything would be a means to an end, everything would be ground up in serving a purpose, and nothing would be worth anything unless we could use it for something else. There wouldn't be anything that we would not be willing to sell if we got a good price. There would be no gift, no grace in life. If we allowed our entire life to be consumed by economies of exchange, by means-ends thinking, if our lives were entirely purpose-driven, we would soon enough find that life had passed us by. We would spend our whole lives saving up for something we never buy.

Our lives would be the butt of the old good news/bad news joke: the good news is we are making excellent time; the bad news is we're lost. So instead of *choosing* between the conditional and the unconditional, it is a matter of *living* between them. The mark of the human condition is to live *in the distance between the conditional and the unconditional,* to constantly negotiate between them.

For me religion means living in constant exposure to the unconditional, open to something excessive, exceptional, unforeseeable, unprogrammable, something slightly mad relative to the rationality of means-and-end thinking. To lack the religion of which I speak is to allow the series of conditions to surround and submerge us. We would see no farther than our noses, have a nose only for a good investment, for making a profit, so that our lives would be consumed by consuming, swallowed up by winning, where everything has a price. As Ecclesiastes might have put it, in our life under the sun, there is a time for calculating and a time not to calculate, to which I would only add: the incalculable is interwoven with the calculable. It is always lingering there, and it may at any moment break out or break through. There are times when we try to measure and foresee, seeking some assurance about outcomes, and then there are things whose immeasurable mystery and obscurity bring us up short and give us pause. These are not actually different things, but different ways of living with things.

Contrary to the assurances of my teachers and religious superiors, the genuine meaning of "eternity" is poetic, not metaphysical. In his famous "Ode on a Grecian Urn," Keats' urn captures the lovers as they are just about to kiss and renders it "eternal," in a kind of freeze frame that allows us to contemplate its "essence." But is it really necessary to add that the lovers would certainly not be content with being held by Keats in eternal suspended animation just before this kiss? That they have other things on their mind? That they want to go all the way? Eternity is an illusion induced by a freeze-frame.

I take traditional religion to be too often beholden to the time of economy, the "economy of salvation," to use theological jargon. Religion too often treats life in time in judicial terms, as a time of trial lived in expectation of an eternal verdict, and in economic terms as a time to make good investments that will pay a big reward, and in metaphysical terms as a time to put time to good use in winning the prize of eternity. Too often religion allows itself to be all about winning, about beating time at its own game, about cheating death. That is religion at its worst. To this I opposed another religion, or another way of being religious, which takes its lead not from winning but from the gift and that interweaves life and death. I embrace a religion of the gift, of an unconditional affirmation made without the expectation of a reward, a religion that we would lack only at our peril.

The great theologian Paul Tillich, the twentieth-century theologian who makes the most sense to me, in an effort to put to rest this endless war—between the believers and the unbelievers, the theists and the atheists, time and eternity, the secular and the religious—said that religion is a matter of "ultimate concern."[8] If you asked Tillich where you might find such religion, he would have said anywhere: in the work of art, in political action, in personal life, wherever there are matters that concern us deeply. That is why the Tillichians sometimes use the expression "secular theology," meaning the theology embedded in the secular, in the *saeculum*, in the times, in time. Religion can happen anywhere—God can happen anywhere—even and especially in the quotidian and so-called secular order. That is very close to what I mean. I would only rephrase it slightly.

Religion, I would prefer to say, is a *matter of unconditional affirmation.* There are times when we affirm things because they are necessary conditions for something else that is required. There are other times when things are affirmed unconditionally, without regard to a payback, be it long term or short term, without regard even to our personal best interests or safety, things that break in upon our comfort zone and interrupt the steady state we try to maintain. Food is necessary as fuel for our bodies; but a common meal with family or friends is a way to say yes to life unconditionally, without regard to fueling up. The unconditional is the salt of the earth; without it our lives turn to dust in our mouth. It is upon this excess, this unconditionality, that a certain religionless religion leaves its trace, and it is that trace whose path I am following here.

Too often pastors and theologians behave like the stockbrokers of eternity, advising their clients on the best investments, competing with other religions over who offers the best deal. The mysticism of the rose proceeds under exactly the opposite presuppositions: that life, this mortal life, is a gift to be savored for itself, that blossoms because it blossoms. This bloom is not waylaid by death, not undermined by mortality, but constituted by it. Life is made all the more precious by its transient beauty, by its fleeting moment in the sun. Life is life/death, living on, outliving death for a time, and the "economy of salvation" is life's worst enemy.

Where the Believers Are

One of the things I observed as I slowly emerged from my pre-Vatican II world, where things were all or nothing, Catholic or not, theist or not, was that people like Lyotard, who have no interest in religion, or like Nietzsche, who said "God is dead" and who could not think of things mean enough to say about religion, very often have deep insights into religion, so long as we are not parsimonious or provincial about what we mean by religion. One of the heroes of my early Catholicism, Hans Küng, ran afoul of the Curia precisely because he repeatedly pointed this out and insisted that religious people who think in terms of inerrancy and infallibility are dangerous. The critics of religion have insights into life, and religion is a form of life. I grew up in a world where I would have thought people like Lyotard were sent into the world by the devil. I gradually came to see that they often touch upon the very nerve of religion, the grace of religion, a religion of grace, a kind of proto-religion, at the least, a religion without religion.

We can see this when Lyotard taunts all those skeptical atheistic naturalistic philosophers who think they do not believe in religion. "You, the unbelievers," he says (with a grin), "You're really believers; you believe too much in that smile"—in "the smile on the surface of matter in a remote corner of the universe."[9] Even the atheists are believers and share in this "euphoria." The professor and I would say now that Lyotard is proposing a religion of the smile, or what with Angelus Silesius we might call the mysticism of the rose. We are all believers in that smile—theists or atheists, innocents or skeptics, physicists or mystics—whatever the differences are that break out among us in our endless debates about the interpretation of the smile.

Like it or not, Lyotard is very effectively evoking a sense of the human in the midst of the inhuman—where the Earth is not a planet in motion but the soil that sustains our step, the moon not simply a terrestrial satellite but something lovers moon over; in this world brooks can be brooding, mountains majestic, and the heavens are full of gods. The poetic drift of his discourse is a strength, not an objection, and is actually a more rigorous way of speaking of what he has in mind.

Lyotard's "smile" incarnates the mysticism of the rose. He might have chosen another figure to the same effect—say, a song sounding in a cosmic void, or a dance performed unseen, off in a remote corner of the universe—and then described believing in that song or joining in that dance. Or he might have cited the lilies of the field, drawing upon one of the sayings of Jesus, one of my favorite Jewish poets (Matt. 6:28). This rose, these lilies, this smile, this song or dance, are all so many occasions for and emblematic figures of terrestrial euphoria. His choice of the smile captures the resilience of the human in the midst of the inhuman, and it reminds us of what Nietzsche called our "golden laughter" in the face of life's recurrent sorrows, which is also a very powerful image.

A smile is a diminutive form of laughter,[10] laughter with discretion, without disturbing anyone else with our outburst. The smile is a silent affirmation of life, a subtle embrace of life, a weak force strong enough to sustain life and give it hope. To smile when it is impossible to smile—what greater strength is there than that? What better example of a power without force or violence? It is like forgiving when it is impossible to forgive, as when Jesus forgives his executioners. What greater strength is there than to smile through our tears? To smile is to say yes to life, yes,

yes, I will, yes, as Molly Bloom said so seductively in her magnificent soliloquy.[11] The smile is the rose of the world, the grace that settles over the world, embodying all three graces—brightness, good cheer, and bloom—in a delicate and gentle gesture. An unsmiling religion is anti-religion; the smile is a religionless religion, which does very well without an unsmiling religion.

Religion, on this accounting, is the doxology of the smile, the guardian of its euphoria, the study of its anatomy. Tracing the anatomy of that smile, mapping the dynamics of its lines of force, articulating the sense it has for us, the highs and lows of the euphoria it induces, that is my subject matter. After spending a lifetime inside and outside religion, trying to deal with it and trying to do without it—that, I am now proposing, is what this thing we call religion is all about. That what's going on in religion. We can even retread the old (and dubious) etymology of the word *religion*, binding-back (*re* + *ligare*), to support Lyotard's cause. Let us say that religion is a way of being bound back to this cosmic smile, not in the sense of creating an economic debt but by way of returning its smile, with a joyous affirmation of the world that greets a smile with a smile. Religion is a doxology of the glory of the smile.

The believers in my religion believe in that smile. Religion does not dig a wormhole into eternity but settles more deeply into time. Becoming religious is a matter of learning how to smile. The smile gives us grounds for hope, albeit groundless grounds, for hoping against hope, for smiles can turn into frowns, and laughter into tears, which means that hope, an audacious hope, knows how to smile through our tears. This smile does not last forever, but that does not refute the smile; it makes it all the more precious.

The rock-bottom nonbelievers, on this telling, have given up on the smile, have been beaten down by life, and they dwell in the depths of despair and depression, having lost the power to smile through their tears. But even then they give negative testimony to the smile, to a certain believing *in* the smile in their very being unable to summon it up. Their despair bears a privative witness to the smile in just the way a man running headlong from a bear bears vivid testimony to the reality of the bear. On that accounting, the only real nonbelievers are the dead—or those who are as good as dead, those who despair, who have the sickness-unto-death. Lacking hope is not a postmodern condition, it is a postmortem condition. Religion has completely disappeared only in the inhuman condition, where there is no smile and no witness to that smile, where matter has lost its smile and there is no one there to report it or return it anyway.

I have done a certain amount of writing myself and I cannot resist the impression that throughout this discourse on the end of time Lyotard himself is having a good time. I see him grinning from ear to ear the whole time he is writing this unnerving essay. He is unable to conceal a smile at these unbelievers who believe after all. We may even detect a bit of a smirk. Might he be entertaining the illusion that he himself is exempt from the ineluctable fate he is writing about in virtue of the fact that he is the one doing the writing? He seems to position himself in the place of an immortal, like a doctor breaking the bad news to the patient (as if the doctor were going to live forever). His readers, on the other hand, are put in the position of a being told about a terrible fate they behold with horror. As the author of the passage, he is able to take a certain amount of enjoyment in what we are all supposed to recognize is a catastrophe, a cataclysm, an apocalyptic ending. He is pleased with himself because he knows very well that his thought of the absolutely unthought is extremely thought-provoking. This essay is a good day's work and another contribution to the smile on the surface of matter— and he knows that. Oblivion is a terrible fate. But the *thought* of oblivion, of the death of death, sends a shiver down our spine and makes us tingle with the life of thought. There is a certain joy in trying to think something joyless and unthinkable.

I am prepared to say that once we shed the shackles too often imposed by the confessional religions, Lyotard is a philosopher of grace. His nihilism is bound up with what I am calling the nihilism of grace, the grace that is granted by looking nihilism in the eye, an audacious cosmic-nihilistic "grace," a word I dare to swipe from the toolbox of classical religion, here refitted do service in our incredulous, postmodern world. Think of the nihilism of grace as depending on the power of nothingness, something that is because it is, nothing more, without why. This nihilism not only dares to think, which is the Enlightenment's audacity, but dares to hope in the blossoming of the rose, which is a mystical audacity, a second and still higher audacity. It dares to smile, which does not mean I am not deadly serious. I am, after all, addressing the question of the inhuman, of cosmic nihilism, of religion and the possibility of hope. There's nothing more serious than that.

It is just as well that I never thought any of this when I was growing up. Had I brought any of it up with the priests or nuns or my religious superiors, they would have shown me the door sooner than I found it myself. But I like to think that I was feeling around in the dark for something like this. I am sure Jackie and Brother Paul would have been scandalized. I think that I would have scared me then.

CHAPTER THREE

How Not to Give a Gift

In one of the books I was assigned to read in the Novitiate, *The Imitation of Christ*, the author Thomas à Kempis says he would rather be humble than know the definition of humility. Talk about creating unnecessary difficulties! Why do I have to choose between them? Brother Paul and I particularly disliked that book, and with good reason. I could not imagine what it had to do with the lively, intelligent men who were my high school teachers, who managed to do both. This disconnect was also a good indication of what was askew in the Novitiate system that prevailed in the Catholic religious orders in those days; it was preparing monks when it should have been preparing members of the active orders. The book was of a piece with the Council of Trent Catholicism in which I grew up, the climate, the atmosphere, the culture, the images, the priests and popes, the holy cards, the holy water, the Holy Family, holy, holy, holy, *sanctus, sanctus, sanctus,* every Sunday morning at Mass, not to mention the other "holydays of obligation," all in Latin, mumbled by a priest whose back was turned to us.

Dare to think? Just you dare! Such audacity was put down by nuns who, called us "bold brazen articles." I don't mean to be misleading. Our nuns were devout and unselfish, hardworking and overworked women, and living on the short end of the Church's patriarchical system. Today, the nuns are the only ones with the nerve to speak out. But it was the 1950s. So, no questions. Until there was one, the same one, then and now, in my dreams no less than in my waking hours. The question for me has always been about God. From the beginning, every other question leading up to God, or in headlong flight from God. How to speak of God? How *not* to speak of God (when God was all I ever heard about)?[1] How to speak of anything else?

Eventually, in a professorial and unapologetically unorthodox voice, I came to speak about what is going on in the name of God, thereby becoming one of the very heretics about whom the *Imitation* was warning the novices. Eventually, to the chagrin of Jackie and the surprise of Brother Paul I was led—by the devil, the Church would say—to the truth of a certain heresy, to the heresy of a certain truth that I discovered—unless it discovered me—having started reading the philosophers, the very ones that so frightened Thomas à Kempis.

To advance the cause of the unorthodox idea of God to which I have been led, to lead you into the same temptation, my plan is this. In the next three chapters (3–5), I will take up two common experiences, giving a gift and offering hospitality, which I claim resonate with the mystical depth of the unconditional. Then, unless my nerve fails me, I will marshal these experiences as evidence in the case I make about God (chapter 6), who is by common agreement the most unconditional thing (or non-thing, or no-thing) of all. All this to see if I can finally settle my accounts with the stars. I am the last one to deny that this is uncertain and risky business, so I am not guaranteeing anything to Jackie, to Brother Paul, or to any of the others who show up every night for my nocturnal seminars.

Let us begin with the unconditionality of the gift.

Giving without Return

When we give a gift, we should by common consent not have anything up our sleeve. In that sense, gifts ought to be "pure," free of any expectation of a payback. That means that the pure gift is not only a good *example* of living without why, it comes very close to being simply what "without why" *means*.

Gifts, of course, are positively famous for being impure. On the side of the recipients, they are well known for their power of corruption, which is why we try to ban giving gifts to politicians and judges and other people in power. Gifts win influence, creating obligations and IOUs to be collected later. On the side of the benefactors, even the most well-intentioned and generous donors cannot resist having their name inscribed on their gifts, on "their" buildings, foundations, scholarships, and endowments. Benefactors are busy people, but they can always find the time to pose for a portrait, rewarding themselves generously for their show of generosity. And they are often made unhappy if their gifts are not used to serve their own purposes by the recipients. I once gave a lecture attended by the benefactor of the (named) lecture series who gave me a hard time for not advancing the conclusions he thought he had paid for in advance! I told him he paid for the questions, not the answers. Indeed, the anthropologists describe "potlatch" competitions about who can give the bigger, splashier gift.[2] Even when a gift we give is greeted with ingratitude we speedily and secretly congratulate ourselves for giving to an ungrateful wretch who does not recognize the depths of our generosity.

That is why Jesus says that gifts are to be given in secret, hidden from the eyes of the world (Matt. 6:1-4). Still, one wonders—with a wonder that would have earned me my walking papers from my parish school and would have so scared me that the thought never crossed my mind—if this saying is not compromised when Jesus goes on to say that if we defer collecting our rewards here on earth, these good deeds will earn an even greater return in heaven when the Father who sees what we do in secret will reward us. There lies the further question: Are pure gifts not also annulled by accruing heavenly rewards? Is the purity of the gift not contaminated when it is turned into a coin redeemable for rewards in an economy of exchange, even if the economy is celestial? Has the time come to say goodbye to heavenly rewards?[3]

Like everything else that is truly interesting and valuable, the gift is built on a dilemma, but its fabric is strengthened by these internal tensions, not destroyed. The dilemma is that

once the gift is recognized as a gift, once an identifiable someone is intentionally and visibly generous to a recipient, the gift
begins to be annulled—donors (who are supposed to be giving
up something) swell with pride in their generosity while recipients (who are supposed to be gaining something) sink under the
weight of the debt of gratitude. The bigger the gift, the deeper
the dilemma. Gifts can be pure poison. Gifts are self-annulling;
donations are auto-detonating, because they set off an "economic" chain reaction, a chain of debts to a manifestly generous
benefactor, try as we may to avoid it:

> I want you to have this gift.
> Thank you. I will never be able to repay you for your
>   generosity.
> I don't want you to repay me. I want you to enjoy this
>   gift.
> I will never forget it.
> Forget it. Take it. It's yours. Enjoy.
> I'll be forever in your debt.
> I don't want you to be in my debt. I want you to have
>   this gift.
> You are wonderfully generous.
> I am not trying to be generous. I am just trying to give
>   this to you.
> I will let everyone know what a generous benefactor
>   you are.
> I am not trying to become famous. How can I convince
>   you? All I want is for you to have this. (Etc.!)

The paradoxical outcome of this dilemma is that the pure
gift would be found only where no one knows that anyone gave

anyone anything. The pure gift does not exist. Let us say that it "insists"—watch this term. I will deploy it throughout to mean something that does not quite exist but still makes itself felt; something that calls upon us, lure us, solicits us. That is very closely tied up with the little heresy that is fomenting in my mind about God that I will spring on you shortly. The pure gift hovers over us like a spirit whispering "Give" in our ear. Or if you prefer, as a specter haunting us, asking us to give without return, to live without a why, while we know full well that such a thing can never actually be found. The pure gift insists; it is up to us to see that it exists. How? By giving. Make it happen, provide it with existence in the real world—knowing all the while that it is bound eventually to turn into another albeit wider and more generous economic circle. Its impossibility is no excuse not to give!

The pure gift calls; we respond. Is that a duty? A categorical imperative? No, no! When it come to the pure gift there must not be any *must*. The gift ought not to have an *ought*.[4] The first law of the gift, like the first law of love, is that the gift, like love, is given without why, without law or duty or debt. If love is given as a duty, it is something less than gracious, something less than love, something less than a gift. If you love me because you must, well then, frankly, I'd rather you not bother. Call it your duty but please don't call it love. Maybe commanded love needs a special name, like love with an asterisk. I would say it is love without a smile. When it comes to love, thou shalt not say thou shalt. It ought not be a duty, indeed it must not. A commanded smile is usually pretty phony, like a politician smiling for a camera, and we all know very well that one can smile while having evil on one's mind. So as beautiful as gifts may be, we also have reason to beware of gift-givers, for they may have a very good reason for their gifts.

The pure gift is a dream, but not an idle one—if we do not dream, reality will be a nightmare—nor is it as entirely exceptional a situation as we might think. Like many other teachers I can tell you of students many years later thanking me for having one day said something in class that stuck with them, that maybe even changed their life. The student did not realize it at the time, and the teacher does not remember having said it—truth to tell, the teacher is struggling even to remember the student. The pure gift remains under the radar of our conscious goals and intentions. It sustains itself in a field of anonymity. Once it becomes visible, intentional, it begins to annul itself. The challenge is to avoid setting off an infinite chain reaction, an infinite debt of unrequitable gratitude and unrepayable obligations on the part of the recipient and of donors swelling with pride in their own generosity.

Once again, we need to recall that it is never a question of choosing between the concrete and conditioned world and the unconditional gift that interrupts it, but of living between them, of inhabiting the distance between them. The gift that is given in the classroom situation would never happen unless there were teachers who are paid a just wage and teacher contracts, school boards and taxes, and buildings kept in good repair. Gifts need economies and are grafted upon them or settle within their cracks. But if all there were to teaching were the school boards and contractual obligations—were there no moments of excess in which everyone (teachers, students, parents, school boards, administrators, and taxpayers) exceed what they are obligated to do—the schools would be a nightmare and no one would learn anything. So if gifts need economies, economies likewise need gifts. Gifts are free, but they are needed. We need people who need to do what they do not need to do. That dilemma is not to be resolved but embraced, because it is how gifts happen.

If we move beyond the classroom and think of the whole world as the "gift of creation," that gift above all others should be given *pro bono*. For then the stakes are so much higher. The threat carried by an infinite gift like creation is to create an infinite obligation, in which every moment of the gift is consumed in returning the gift, in sending endless hosannas up to the Infinite, Omnipotent, and Omnibenevolent Benefactor in the sky who wants his name inscribed on everything. If, God forbid, we were to offend that Infinite Benefactor, then God help us; there would be no way to pay him (sic) back. That reduces religious liturgies to the status of a television commercial, and their magnificent hymns to jingles, where a Sabbath time is set aside for a word from our sponsor who made all this possible. If creation is a gift, it should run free of commercial interruption. If the world is a gift, then we are invited to rejoice in our time in the world.

It is precisely here, just at this point of infinite gifts, that the eyes of religion grow large—for it sees that there are huge profits to be made. Some religious people behave like capitalists shouting "Greed is good!"—they can tell when there's a celestial buck to be made, and they are, as Lacan said, "fabulous" at doing just that. Insinuating himself into the situation of the gift, all garbed in black, his unsmiling eyes cast heavenwards, his reverence announces solemnly that by being born we have incurred an infinite debt and are bound (*ligare*) to give infinite thanks back (*re*) to our Infinite Benefactor in the sky and to make infinite reparations to him (sic) for offending his generosity. Thereby does his reverence seize with no little success upon an opportunity to earn a profitable living for himself from a gift. Here is where religion too often gets its funding.

Such religion annuls the gift, darkens the smile on the face of matter, scatters the petals of the rose, mocks the lilies of the field, and raises an important question about just what is going on in such religion. Above all, it raises a question about what is going on in the name of God in such religion, the big question toward which I am slowly inching a cautious path, without trying to drive my more conservative friends from the room. If I were one of these medieval copyists who dared to tinker with the scriptures they were copying,[5] I'd insert a little dialogue in the beginning of Genesis in which, after declaring creation good seven times, Elohim adds, "Take it, it's yours. Don't thank me. Enjoy!" I would then inscribe a hymn to a gratitude without gratitude, a gracious ingratitude, which consists in flourishing in the grace of the given gift. They would never stand for any such shenanigans back in the diocesan Chancery Office.

A Hitherto Lost Scroll

I will tell you a secret. Ever since I first heard of the Dead Sea Scrolls, I have been dreaming, praying, lighting candles in every chapel I pass, all in hope that someone will discover just one more scroll, even just a fragment of a scroll, tucked away under a rock in one of those caves that will give my religion without why or wherefore a firm scriptural foundation and endow it with unshakeable certitude. I have almost given up hope. The years are rushing by, and I have reached the point where I may simply have to forge it. Announcing such a discovery may be my only chance to make the cover of *Time* magazine as the death-of-God theologians did years ago, or to make some headlines like the people in the Jesus Seminar. If one day you find yourself reading in the newspapers of my discovery of a fragment from a lost gospel, you will know what I have been up to, so I ask you for your discretion. My missing manuscript will contain a variant version of a familiar pericope:

> *Servant*: Lord, when we did we feed you when you were hungry—we never even heard of you?
>
> *Lord*: You have not heard of me because I do not exist. I insist.
>
> *Servant*: Lord, when did we clothe you when you were naked? We never laid eyes on you.
>
> *Lord*: You never saw me because I do not exist, but I call upon you night and day.
>
> *Servant*: Lord, while I have you on the line—I was on hold for a really long time, it felt like forever—I have been meaning to ask you, what is your name?
>
> *Lord*: I have as many names as I need, depending on the time and place, depending on the need, and no one needs to know any one particular name. You only need to know that your needs are my needs. I can happen anywhere.
>
> *Servant*: I get all that, but still we need to call you something.
>
> *Lord*: I cannot be contained by one name. I have no one name in particular. Tell the denominations that I am

non-denominational, *de*-nominational. I am subject to no one-name-fits-all nomination. In fact, it's worse than that. I am more verbal than nominal, more adverbial than verbal, more prepositional, adjectival than anything, and depending on how far you want to go with this, my trace is to be found in the diacritical marks. I am in the space between the words, the breath marks of the Masoretes. I am a matter of the *how* not the *what*.

Servant: But then, Lord, who is the giver of all good things?

Lord: The pure gift is given without a giver, given even without cognizance of a gift, where the only gratitude is not to realize that anyone is owed thanks.

Servant: Just one last thing, Lord, and I promise you this is the last question. I know you are busy, but this one really eats at me: What is the resurrection of the dead?

Lord: A newborn baby, a new morning, another day, more time, a recovery from a mortal threat, a remission, a repetition, making a leap when it is impossible to move an inch, a comeback, a second chance, a new . . .

There the manuscript breaks off. I would then report that scholars offer that there are reasons to believe the fragment is part of a long-lost gospel that has been speculatively reconstructed under the name of a so-called "G-Gospel," to which there are occasional but highly oblique references in manuscript fragments of several other obscure ancient authorities. Anglophone scholars assume this means the "Gospel of the Gift," but a recent study shows that it was first hypothesized was by a nineteenth-century German scholar, which changes everything![6]

My imaginary G-Gospel refers to one of the most beautiful texts found in the New Testament, the story of the servants who are blessed by the master for their service—precisely when *they did not know* it was the master they were serving or that there were rewards in store for their good deeds. The master is anonymous, the gift is concealed in non-knowing, and the servants did what they did without the idea of winning the master's favor. This story is another lovely presentation of the purity of gift, where the gift is a gift if it is given unconditionally, without ulterior motives, freely, without why, without regard to a reward or recompense. Here, *inside* religion, in a canonical text of Christianity, is a religionless Christianity, a religion drawing upon the resources of the mysticism of the rose while testifying to the *outside*. Here, in a story about the economy of salvation, of eternal rewards and punishments, this parable tells us to live without why.

Mercy without Mercenaries

One of the things that moved me to embrace the religious life was the prospect of a life spent teaching young people, making a difference in their lives, and doing so without the slightest interest in how much money was to be made. This was not to be a "career," a line of work, but a "vocation." Religion inspires people to do things like that all the time. A few years ago I was having dinner with an old friend of mine who described himself to me as a "lapsed Catholic." This took me by surprise. It would have been an otherwise unremarkable observation— I think I know more lapsed than unlapsed Catholics—but for the fact that my friend was a member of a Catholic religious order. When I asked him how this worked, he said that while he observes his duties as a member of the order, including daily Mass, down deep he believes he no longer really believes any of it. I asked the obvious question. Then why don't you leave the order? Because, he said, his real vocation is the children, with or without the backup theology of the Church. He works with children who have seen more trouble in their young lives than most of us do in a lifetime and, knowing this man, I am sure he works wonders with them. That, I said to him in response, sums up in a strikingly simple way a lot of what I am writing about, usually in a much more complicated way. He is making the kingdom of God come true because these children *are* the kingdom of God—with or without God.

This is a salutary warning to those of us who like to give religion a hard time. Truth to tell, were a ruthless age of secularization to overwhelm us resulting in the wholesale closing of religious institutions everywhere, we would suddenly find ourselves in short supply of people to run the schools and hospitals, shelters for the homeless, food kitchens and medical clinics in the most desperate neighborhoods, relief workers who continue to serve the victims of natural disasters long after the TV cameras and journalists have gone home and the story has lost its novelty. We would, in short, be deprived of countless works of mercy and of the unselfish service of the wretched of the earth, of the poorest and most defenseless people in society, labors that by and large fall to religious people.

So when Jacques Lacan mocks the ability of priests who know how to come up with the illusory consolations of eternal rest, honesty dictates that he include all these works of mercy in the list of things he is mocking. When the secular left cites Marx's mockery of religion as the opium of the people, honesty dictates that they also cite the rest of that same passage, in which Marx speaks of religion as the heart of a heartless world— once again, an atheist touches upon the very nerve of religion— as a practice meant to bring relief to the victims of heartless capitalist greed. Marx thought that the religious heart faithfully records the sighs of the oppressed, keeping a record of an injustice that he thought called for a remedy, not with more religion, of course, but with real, economic justice.[7]

These concrete works of mercy are salient examples of the purity of the gift, of works of mercy blossoming like the rose, without regard to whether anyone knows they are there. In biblical terms, these practices make up the reality, the actuality, the existence of the kingdom of God, a kingdom that is always coming and never quite exists. In the language of the Apostle Paul, they fill up what is lacking in the body of Christ (Col. 1:24). In my professorial terms, they supply the existence that is lacking in insistence.

My idea is not to beat religion senseless but to claim that religion is constantly getting in its own way by its built-in tendency to shrink down the unconditional gift (which is the religion in religion) into an economic exchange. It allows itself to be led into the temptation to turn works of mercy into coins in the realm of the economic system of the kingdom of God. In this world virtue goes unrequited; but in the next one we will be rich as hell—or rather heaven. When these works of mercy have that religion up their sleeve, by which I mean the economy of salvation, that is not the gift. The relief packages are distributed as part of a package deal put together by the proselytizers who make it clear that these are not just works of mercy. These works are also the work of celestially minded mercenaries, works with mercenary value. That is literally true, as Matthew speaks of the celestial rewards (*merces*) awaiting those who do these works in secret and are willing to wait for heaven to be rewarded (Matt. 6:1-6). That reduces the gratuity of their grace to a delayed gratification. Then the agents of the kingdom of God are like bankers bearing "gifts." They are selling heavenly bonds, promoting the business of religion, part of a religious bait-and-switch game, which attracts the hungry who quickly understand that there is no free lunch.

But in the proto-religion whose cause I am advancing, the works of mercy *are* the kingdom of God; the kingdom of God is not a reward (*mistos, merces*, Matt. 6:1) for doing works of mercy. Religious relief workers have to resist the temptation to become religious mercenaries, where the works of mercy are their tools in trade, and the hungry end up appeasing the hunger of missionaries—for heavenly treasures and converts here on earth.

The story in Matthew 25 about feeding the Son of Man when he was hungry, clothing him when he was naked, and visiting him when he was in prison, while having no idea that this is the Son of Man, is a beautiful illustration of the realization of the purity of the gift of works of mercy. It brings a smile to our lips, as far as it goes. The problem is, it goes farther. We who love this parable often leave out its context. The author of the Gospel has framed this core story within a not-so-beautiful economy of rewards and punishments, by which it is rather severely undermined. It belongs to an account of the coming of the Son of Man on the day of judgment—on the day when the sun and moon are darkened and the stars fall from the sky (Mark 13:25). On that day the Son of Man will separate the sheep from the goats. That is—for those of us urban or suburban types who enjoy goat cheese and who don't see any strong reason to prefer sheep to goats—those who will inherit the kingdom as a reward for good conduct from those who are to be consigned to "the eternal fire prepared for the devil and his angels." That is the sort of thing that leads a lot of people to think that if you do not believe in this system of rewards and punishments, then, short of being caught by the police and locked up, anything goes! These are perfectly good Christians, otherwise lovely people, who do not realize the utterly cynical view this implies of what a human being is.

The image of eternal fire has made quite a lot of confessional theologians understandably nervous, resulting in a recent spate of literature aimed at walking back this bit of orthodox doctrine, either by removing its terrible bite (everybody is saved, hell is empty)[8] or by just rejecting it outright as the cruel (and quite pre-Copernican) myth it is. If the truth be told, it is the most profoundly hateful image to be found in the gospel of love in the New Testament, one that makes a perfect mockery of the image of the God of love that its authors are trying to construct in other passages. The cruelty it fantasizes far exceeds anything a Roman crucifixion could inflict on Jesus, which is over in a matter of hours. Up above, an unsmiling God, arms folded, remains eternally unrelenting, ignoring the howling down below. At this point it becomes impossible to distinguish God from Satan. That is why the visionary poet William Blake said that the transcendent God beyond the world *is* Satan.[9] So the beautiful narrative of Matthew 25 of a merciful God who stands systematically on the side of those who are hungry, naked, imprisoned, and dispossessed, is framed within an image of a merciless Judge. The only thing more astonishing than this incongruity is how regularly it is ignored by those who cite this story as an example of the God of love.

The story is at odds with itself: it recognizes the unconditionality of a gift given under the conditions of anonymity—the pure gift is not recognized as such—which it then proceeds to undermine by entering it into the calculations made by the Son of Man. The conclusion we are meant to draw is clear: You never know if this beggar on the street is the Lord himself, so don't take any chances. Feed the hungry, clothe the naked, visit the imprisoned, anytime, night and day, every time you get the chance. Do not weary in your well doing—the return on your investment will exceed your wildest dreams, and the loss you will otherwise incur will exceed your most terrifying nightmares. No stock investor on Wall Street has ever seen rewards like this.

A lot of theologians today think that theology can do better than that. I dare say, God can do better than that. The God of love should keep an infinite distance from the economy of salvation. The God of love, the giver of all good gifts, "Abba," does not sit on a throne and separate out "his" children—can you imagine a parent like that, separating their sheep children from their goat children, dispensing eternal rewards and punishments? God does not "do" anything at all except to call for mercy, and even then God does not "do" that, as if God were a motivational speaker or a cheerleader on the sidelines. God declines the prestige of presence, of thrones surrounded with fawning angels before which the nations gather to be judged, even if there are plenty of places in the scriptures that embrace that vision.

God, what is going on in the name of God, repels that imperial model with a divine fury, and hates these sacrifices (Amos 5:21-24). The name of God is the name of a call that calls for a response, of an insistence that strains to exist, of a truth that we are asked to make come true *in* these works. The kingdom of

God is not a *reward* for these works; the kingdom *is* these works. The name of God is not the name of agent-judge who rewards and punishes on the basis of these works: it *is* the name of these works. The insistence of God comes to exist *in* these works and *as* these works. The name of God is a fragile flower, a rose easily crushed under the heavy boots of confessional doctrines, by marketing deals sold from the pulpit, and by missionary expeditions profiteering on the misery of the poor, and other versions of celestial economies still to come.[10]

I like to think that Mother Teresa's finest moments were the doubts she endured, those moments when it came over her that she just might not really believe in God or accept any of the doctrines defined by her Catholic faith.[11] What I am drawn to here is not the sight of a good woman suffering but the fact that she never expressed any doubt at all about her *work*, that her works of love fell free of her doctrinal doubts. Here the purity of the gift comes breaking through—for her and for us. Her work stood, with or without God; her work stood, without why. Her work *was* the work of God, which is what the rabbis mean when they speak of loving the Torah more than God. The work of serving the poor and the starving *is* the work of God, the very *body* of God, the *existence* of God in response to God's insistence. What she realized in these moments of doubt and self-questioning is the somewhat irregular thought I have been nurturing, the little heresy I will develop below under the name of the insistence of God, where God insists, and serving the poor in and under the name of God is how God exists.

These days, I fear, I have become a fellow who would have scared poor Jackie half to death.

CHAPTER FOUR

Goodbye Heaven: The Religion of Marguerite and the Big Church

W hen my father died, my mother, a perfectly devout and orthodox Catholic, asked me if I believed she would rejoin my father in heaven one day. I had not the slightest hesitation in saying I did, even though it had been a while since I had believed anything of the sort. But I was not about to disabuse her faith and certainly not at a moment like that. What I really thought was that their life together was whole and holy all by itself, and that the notion of a heavenly reunion was, at worst, a mystification of married life, and at best, a symbolic way of saying their love was as strong as death. In truth, I thought, their love for one another was without why, and did not in any way depend on a fantastic heavenly reunion in incorruptible bodies.

As you can see, I have given up entirely on earning this book an *imprimatur* from the Church. I am signaling a wholly other sort of God, and dreaming of another sort of Church, one that has been stirring in the back of my mind, way back, in the hidden corners of my heart, where for a long time I was afraid to bring it up at the nightly sessions attended by Jackie and the rest of us. But the pattern is emerging of a God who would have landed me in public school. A God who is otherwise, who abdicates the power to punish his enemies with eternal pain and to reward his friends with eternal happiness. These two, both the Prime Punisher and the Royal Rewarder go hand in hand; they come as a package deal in the economy of salvation.

In this chapter, my strategy is to shift the focus from a God who abandons the economy of rewards and punishments to a humanity who abandons any such God. Such a "soul," to use mystic-speak, is audacious enough to bid adieu to such a God (*adieu à Dieu*). Living without the why's and wherefore's of this economy raises the question of living without the Church that has the staff to administer the laws and keep track of the offenders in this economy. I am not trying to get rid of the Church. I am trying to shame one Church by means of another, another move I shamelessly steal from the mystics.

The Big Church and the Little Church

I am referring to the life and mystical writings of Marguerite Porete (d. 1310)—one of the greatest of the Beguines, a suspect group of religious women in the Late Middle Ages. As an educated, aristocratic, and fiercely independent laywoman, Marguerite clearly caught the Church by surprise. Porete authored a book titled *The Mirror of Simple Souls* (a woman writing anything was an unwelcome surprise to the Church).[1] By "simple" she meant living with the naked purity of the gift, "without why," an expression she herself employed several times. It is very likely that Meister Eckhart, one of my earliest heroes, first came across this expression in her writings. In this book, which is a dialogue among three protagonists, the Soul, Reason, and Love, Marguerite introduces a distinction between the Little Church and the Big Church. Unfortunately, the Little Church was the one with all the power and carried quite a Big Stick, and so this distinction eventually cost Marguerite her life. So while she left the Church nonplussed, the Church for its part left her worse than that. But she was not one to be intimidated by the Little Church.

The Little Church is governed by Reason, by which she did not mean what the Enlightenment meant by "pure reason," but what we have been calling an "economy of exchange," a system of *quid pro quo*. In the sphere of Reason, everything we do has a "why," a reason, an end, be it terrestrial or celestial. So Reason for her is like what is called nowadays "means-end rationality," behaving like a rational utilitarian, but with this big difference: she included spiritual matters in its calculations. She did not know anything about utilitarianism, but she did know something about Aristotle, who said that every agent acts for an end, for the sake of its own good, its own "why," even if it be a misguided end or merely apparent good.[2]

The reign of Reason extends over the world of space and time, the visible and sensible world, which means that the Church here on earth is governed by Reason. The Little Church is all about the reasonable business of the Church. That is pretty much the one that Jackie, Brother Paul, and I grew up in, the visible Church: the administration buildings, the catechisms, the Mass and Sacraments, the Latin, the priests and nuns, what we all simply called, without question and not without a little fear and trembling, "the Church." The only ecclesiastical distinction we knew was not between Big and Little, but between "One, True, Catholic and Apostolic" and Protestant. In speaking of the Little Church, Marguerite meant that while it is big and powerful in all the ways I experienced as a youngster, it is spiritually little. We called it "holy mother, the Church," and none of us thought or called it "little"! For Marguerite the Little Church included not simply its administrative offices and buildings, magnificent cathedrals, and long-robed prelates, but also the economic system of sacraments, the hierarchy, the Apostles themselves, the invitation to practice the vows of poverty, chastity, and obedience, and even (the historical) Jesus. The Little Church administers an economy of salvation. It has bricks and mortar, computers and bureaucrats, an administrative staff and a treasury, a creed to recite, sacraments to receive, canon law, cult, and theological councils. What she is describing sounds like the diocesan world overseen by the Cardinal Archbishop in which I grew up, after whom we have since named a high school and a road! In short, the Little Church is in no short supply of either terrestrial or celestial power, which is why back in the day popes could bring emperors to their knees.

Here's the key to the Little Church: if you keep the Ten Commandments, practice the four cardinal virtues, add in the three theological virtues and—if you really want the platinum package—top it all off with the three counsels of perfection (poverty, chastity, and obedience); if you do all twenty things (count them), your heavenly rewards will be countless. My children sometimes asked what (in heaven's name!) made me choose a life in a religious order, that decision being completely incomprehensible to them. The answer is simple: do the numbers. I thought my friends who chose to remain "in the world" were walking away from a good deal. The life the Brothers led was appealing in both terrestrial (I loved the idea of a life of teaching) and celestial terms (I was just a beginner, on the lowest stratum of Marguerite's ladder of perfection!) Street-smart people go into currency exchange, but heaven-smart souls, doing a little heavenly-cloud-computing, find their treasure in prayer and Mass and the Sacraments, and in countless good works. They thereby lay up for themselves an eternal reward, while the goods the street-smart investors have piled up are exposed to moths and rust (Matt. 6:20). Ultimately the children of the light are a lot smarter than the children of the world. In the Little Church, everything has a "why." In their purpose-driven life, the purpose is *beatitudo*, bliss, the vision of God, eternal happiness. Absent such practices, the results are dire—beyond rust and moths, fire, hell, and damnation.[3] We speak of the folly of the cross and being fools for Christ. But people in the Little Church are not fools, not in the long term. They know exactly what they are doing and where their best interests lie. They know that religion is good business.

The Big Church, on the other hand, is governed by Love, by what we have been calling the "gift," an expenditure made without an expectation of a return. In this realm everything is done without why. The Big Church is made up of the community of what Marguerite calls simple or an*nihil*ated souls, souls bent on nothing, on becoming nothing, doing things for nothing. The mystics have considerable commerce with the nothing, about whose unsayability they have volumes to say. So if this is a form of "being," it is being-for-nothing, which means of course, nothing further, nothing else, nothing up our sleeve, and no long robes. I am stealing my idea of nihilism from the mystics. For it is in this annihilated soul that we see the makings of the nihilism of grace. The soul is simple when it is empty and naked, divesting itself of all its assets, disinvesting itself of everything that occupies the time of the souls in the Little Church. It strips itself of its own will, detaches itself from its "virtues," these twenty spiritual adornments, making itself free and disencumbered of temporal and spiritual merchandise, returning itself to the pure and simple way it preexisted in the divine mind before it was created, going back to its factory-settings.

To live by love is to live "without why," for love loves without seeking after some good in return for the love. A return may come, but that is not why we love. So Marguerite is making use of the distinction the other Jackie makes between "economy" and the "gift," which we explored in the previous chapter. In the Little Church, the soul is always after something, always striving, always willing and desiring, doing this and doing that in search of a heavenly reward. All such seeking after is for Marguerite at bottom so much self-seeking, a soul seeking its own happiness, where there is a thin line between wanting to go to heaven and narcissism. In the Big Church, the simple soul is stripped naked of the vestments and investments made by the self, living what Meister Eckhart called a life of "releasement" (*Gelassenheit*) and "detachment" (*Abgeschiedenheit*), a word that means both *cut off* and *departed*—even *dead*. We spent a lot of time in our Novitiate reading about detachment and death to the world. We spent even more time trying to practice it around the monastic clock—but not without why. If someone told me this was all without why, my bags would have been packed before the next stroke of the clock. We were doing this *for* such a time when there would be no time or clocks. I had not considered the twist Marguerite was giving detachment. By saying goodbye to the self-seeking of both worldly *and celestial* goods, the simple soul resides in a palace of divine union, having bid adieu to the tireless devotions, works, and virtues of life in time—that is, of "religion." Marguerite's simple soul does without all this religion and even, as a Beguine, without joining an officially approved religious order, which would have given her an ecclesiastical status.

The Little Church is religion; the Big Church is a religion without religion.

The result is that the "annihilated" soul has become nothing in the sense of living *for*-nothing-else. The simple soul does not seek the kingdom of God, not because she seeks something *else*, but because she does not *seek* anything. Here is where we need to be cautious. Marguerite says this not because she is an atheist and does not believe in heaven. She says it because the kingdom of God is nothing to be sought, and this because, as Jesus said, it is already within us. It does not come after, because it is now. Like St. Paul, the simple soul can say that it lives now not I but Christ lives in me (Gal. 2:20). The soul does not strive for

God as for an external good but lives "from out of the experience"[4] of union with God and so bids adieu to God. The simple
soul, accordingly, bids adieu, goodbye, farewell, to the virtues,
which are end-directed activities conducted under the rule of
Reason. For the simple soul, God is not its final goal but its
beginning; union with God is not acquired in the end but is
present from the beginning, as that from which all life begins,
even as it presses in upon us in the present. To bid adieu to the
virtues is to say farewell to end-driven and self-seeking practices.
This leads Marguerite to scoff at "feeding the virtues until they
are fat," adorning ourselves with virtues like a politician running
television commercials advertising his good works. The simple
soul, on the other hand, is lean and clean, empty of self and full
of God, and would have a hard time winning an elected office.

In detaching itself from Reason and the "economy of salvation," from the system of rewards and punishments, the soul
is even—and this is the extreme point of what she means by
its "simplicity"—detached from heaven and hell. This leads to
a trope to be found in Marguerite and Eckhart in which the
simple soul is so filled with the love of God's will and stripped
of its own will that it would be all the same to the soul were it
to be condemned to hell for all eternity. So long as that were,
per impossibile—that's why it is a trope—God's will. Goodbye
virtue, goodbye heaven.[5] No wonder she had piqued the curiosity of the Curia.

In Marguerite's view, the virtues to which she bids adieu
belong within an economic scheme where everything is ordered
to an end, an eschatology, where the end is eternal beatitude. This
was an adaptation of Aristotelian teleology (the logic of "ends,"
telos), where every action is oriented toward its goal or good,

where no one does anything unless there is a good to be attained. Of course that doesn't guarantee that they are right about what they think is good, which is why some goods are only apparent goods. But either way, what they are after is "happiness."

Marguerite renounces beatitude inasmuch as it represents an end external to the will. Kant insisted that we do our duty for duty's sake, not for the sake of being happy. But Marguerite's objection is not Kant's. Her objection is that a certain beatitude is already given. The end is already in the beginning. The end has already begun right now, in an anticipatory way, in the life led by the simple soul right here on earth. But life on earth is a vale of tears, beset on every side by trials and sorrows. So the earthly life of the simple soul is at best a life of steely joy in the midst of sorrow that can blossom fully and unencumbered only in eternity. Then the soul is released from time and tears and even from the corruptible body itself at death. Joy means the power to smile through our tears here on earth; in heaven, time and its tears will be wiped away.

The saints and mystics bought themselves a considerable amount of trouble precisely by denying that love can be bought or sold. At times Marguerite seems not far from saying something even more audacious, that she prefers to be damned rather than to be united with a God who would permit such a thing as hell in the first place. For saying things this beautiful and audacious, Meister Eckhart was condemned while Marguerite, who did not have the advantage of being a male, a famous friar, or a respected master of theology, was burned at the stake. These great mystics were made to pay dearly for their love of the gift. They dared to say that love is a gift and that it is corrupted by cutting deals, and they dared to decline being a party to this deal. The Little

Church had little tolerance for such audacity, little love for pure love, and took a most ungenerous attitude toward the pure gift. Unfortunately for her (and for the Church), the Little Church had all the power. The audacity of love is suffocated by the fury of the God of omnipotence. It is impossible to love someone who threatens infinite punishment if you don't and promises infinite rewards if you do. The Church likes to call itself the bride of Christ, but can you imagine such a marriage? In the courts, they call it spousal abuse; here we say it is love without a smile.

This recalls an old joke: you should marry for love, not for money; it's just easier to love someone rich. Actually, in a religion modeled after the mysticism of the rose, the opposite is true: it's a lot harder.

Quiet without Quietism

As much as I admire the mystics for being outsiders found right inside religion, I am not entirely uncritical of them. I have already pointed out that they have allowed the distinction between the gift and an economy to be submerged in a Greek philosophical distinction between eternity and time. That results in conflating a life lived "without why" with a withdrawal from life in time and the body into the inner stillness of an eternal now. From the point of view of the orthodoxy of the Little Church, this was not so much wrong as too much of a good thing. And too soon; it was jumping the gun, acting as if we lived in eternity already (the Church Triumphant) even while we were still being tossed about in the turmoil of time (the Church Militant).

But this conflation carries along with it another threat, which can be seen in one of the most serious charges by which these mystics were beset, that of quietism. This means a withdrawal not only from the rewards gained for good works but also from good works themselves. Does the simplicity of the soul mean it divests itself from works of mercy, from ministering to the poor and visiting the imprisoned and feeding the hungry? Does it retreat into an inner contemplative quiet that lets the world go to hell in a hand basket? Does being-for-nothing-ism translate on the practical level into do-nothing-ism? This charge cannot be taken lightly. You can see the tension here by considering the life of Thomas Merton, who is one of the luminous figures in my generation of Catholics. We had a full stock of his books in the Novitiate. Merton initially sought out a contemplative life as a Trappist monk, but he grew increasingly impatient with the Church and even with his own monastic life for its silence about all the violence (the nuclear arms race and the Vietnam war) in the world around them.

Marguerite is a particularly puzzling figure on this account. On the one hand, all the accounts we have of her personal life and death portray a woman of steely resolve and uncommon courage, a woman willing to defy a patriarchal Church in life and who in death met her executioners with inner calm, refusing even to acknowledge the authority of the men who held her fate in their hands. It would be exceedingly foolhardy to confuse such inner quiet of soul with quietism. Furthermore, in distinguishing joy from happiness, she made it clear that the mysticism of the rose is no rose garden, that it is not without the thorns and thistles of life in time, a point that she no doubt experienced firsthand in the persecution she suffered at the hands of the Little Church. On this point she differs from Meister Eckhart, who portrays living without why as a scene of such serenity as to seem insulated from all earthly troubles.

On the other hand, while she is a woman of saintly courage and a model for the rest of us, beyond all personal reproach, a certain difficulty persists in what she is saying. The soul becomes simple by passing through three purifications, which she describes as three deaths, each of which gives birth to a new and purer life.[6] The first is the death to sin, to a will that has turned away from God, and this in turn gives birth to the life of grace, which is life according to the teachings of the Little Church, which follows the dictates of Reason and practices the virtues. The second is the death to nature, by which she means marriage, family, career, the good but still ordinary Christian life in the material world, which gives birth to the life of the spirit, by which she means the life of evangelical perfection, of poverty, chastity, and obedience, of spiritual and ascetic acts and contemplative practices. The third and highest death is to the spirit, departing entirely from bodily and created nature, dying not only to bad works but to good works, which gives birth to the divine life of the soul, its life as an "annihilated" soul. This is a state of complete uncreated will-lessness, where it has annihilated its own will and lives entirely in God, bidding adieu to the virtues, indeed to grace, nature, and spirit for entrance into a divine nothingness. Only this third stage is "without why." (It was all Brother Paul and I could do to get into the second stage. That was death enough for us!) These three stages are not entirely unlike a distinction made by Meister Eckhart, who identified three kinds of will: the bad will (disobeys the will of God); the good will (conforms to the will of God), which is higher; and pure will-lessness, the self-annulling will, which is the highest of all.

This ladder of perfection causes some confusion about the status of the rest of the kingdom of God in the third stage, the bit about feeding the hungry and ministering to the least among us, putting off your prayers until after you have settled any disagreement you have with your neighbor. All of this Marguerite seems to consign to the lower, less refined sphere. She was an aristocrat who used class-conscious metaphors, and she had a tendency to look down her mystical nose at her coarser neighbors. The implications of her mystical theology for ordinary life—back down among the "lower class" stages of "grace" and "spirit"—are disconcerting. Is the practice of evangelical works of mercy superfluous? Is the world not filled with souls still poor and naked, or hungry and imprisoned, in a very real and literal sense, the ministry to whom was integral to the preaching of Jesus? Is not love of our neighbors down here in the world of "grace" and "spirit" co-constitutive with the love of God in Jesus' preaching? When he announced his mission, Jesus addressed the most carnal and earthy matters, like being poor and imprisoned, which he called the coming of the kingdom of God. The Kingdom is a thoroughly temporal, carnal matter, a matter of concrete action, what Kierkegaard called the "works of love."

Is there not the threat of another kind of violence here? Not the violence of the Little Church which was persecuting her and anybody else who stepped out of line, but the violent abnegation of the created world, of the world of space and time? Mysticism makes for a perfect storm when it merges with the underlying Neoplatonic philosophy it has swallowed. It treats time as an imperfection, instead of treating it as the affirmative and elemental momentum of our lives that gives us the only chance we have of renewal and rebirth. In the Neoplatonic idea of absolute peace and eternal rest, the ideal of resting in peace, *requiescat in pace*, God and death cut an eerie funereal circle around each other, a veritable dance of death, where real life begins only in the grave. For Marguerite, this ever-vanishing temporal now is the source of our restlessness and unhappiness, which is only abolished in the absolute, imperishable, and eternal now where God and the soul unite. Having conflated the distinction between the economy of "why" and the gift that is given "without why" with a distinction between a temporal striving will and eternal rest, between life in time and eternal life, she seems to leave the works of mercy in distress. The life of Marguerite's simple soul is rest without movement, unity without multiplicity, eternity without time, soul without body. Are we being asked to bid farewell to tending to the temporal, carnal, and corporeal needs of oneself and of others?

It is not clear to me how we are to interpret the texts of Marguerite Porete. I will leave that to the experts.[7] But Meister Eckhart shows us how to steer clear of the problem by way of an unorthodox reinterpretation of the story of the visit paid by Jesus to the home of Mary and Martha:

> Now as they went on their way, he entered a certain village, where a woman named Martha welcomed him into her home. (Luke 10:38)

In the Middle Ages, this story was taken as an allegory of the distinction between the active life and contemplative life. Martha, who scurries about in order to provide for the needs of the divine guest, is the figure of the active life; Mary, who sits adoringly at his feet basking in the divine light, is the figure of the contemplative life; the little village is the figure of the soul to which Jesus seeks to be admitted. In the traditional view, Jesus' gentle rebuke, "Martha, Martha you worry over too many things," signified the superiority of contemplation over action. In saying this, their Jesus was just being a good Aristotelian: union is the end, action is the means to an end. But Meister Eckhart, who was a master of contrarian and figurative interpretations of the Scriptures, said the opposite is the case.[8] Contrary to the literal words of Jesus, the secret or mystical meaning of his words is that Martha chose the better part, for Jesus speaks Martha's name twice, secretly signifying that Martha had two gifts to Mary's one. Martha lived *both* the contemplative and the active life while Mary languished at his feet in adoring love, as if her union with God were too fragile to withstand commerce with the actual world. Because Martha's unity with God was more robust, she could, without cost to the inner grounding of her soul in God, actively engage in ministering to Jesus—sweeping the house in anticipation of his arrival at their home, tending to his needs after he arrived tired and hungry, in need of good food, a place to wash and sleep, and addressing his other bodily needs.

There is a marvelous materialism in Martha's mystical unity with Jesus, and on Eckhart's telling Jesus prefers her materialism to Mary's immaterialism. There is no shrinking from Jesus' animal nature, his animal needs; her theology is a zoo-theology. How is that possible? Because Martha does all this out of the plentitude of her uninterrupted union with Jesus. Martha's good works in the world are not superfluous to her mystical unity with Jesus but their issue. They are what Eckhart calls the *ebullitio*, the welling up and flowing over of the life of God within her out into the world. Her works are not the issue of her own ego in search of rewards but of God's life within her. Martha's works *are* the works of God in the world, what God means in the world, what Jesus promised that the kingdom of God would mean. (In my terms: how God's insistence acquires existence in the world.)

On this interpretation of the figure of Martha, the life of virtue is not suspended in the sense that the soul enters a sphere of will-lessness where virtue is cut off or left behind. It is suspended in the sense that it was re-hung, that the hook on which it hangs is no longer her will but God within her. Action is not stopped up but suspended otherwise, made to swing from another hook. In another place, Eckhart says that the unity of action and contemplation is like a door swinging on the immovable hinge on which it is suspended. The hinge remains still even as the door swings freely. Martha's life of virtue was not hers but God's life within her, and the busy life of the virtues did not distract or dissipate her unity with Jesus. Instead, union with God overflows freely into her engagement in the world. Thus the practice of the works of mercy are neither subordinated to a purpose nor rendered superfluous. They are not a superfluity but an overflowing; they are an excess, not an excision of action. Marguerite's account of the simple soul makes us wonder if she is Mary all the way down, her simplicity meaning she has only one gift, her mystical unity having dealt death to the coarse life of housekeeping and virtue-doing.[9]

In another sermon, Eckhart makes the same point by introducing another figure into the mystical equation, that of the detached soul as both a virgin and a wife.[10] She is a virgin because her love of God is pure of every attachment to finite things, and this includes not only worldly things, like fine clothes or jewelry, but religious things, the pieties of religion, like the smells and the bells, the candles and the religious services, the creedal assertions and "correct" beliefs of religion. But the detached soul is also a wife, fruitful, birth-giving, giving birth to the Son in the soul, in the world, which are the works of mercy and of love. That figure of fertility, I think, trumps the Neoplatonic thematics of death—both the "death of God" and the death of the "annihilated" soul. Whatever we finally come to think God means, it must include life, more life.

CHAPTER FIVE

Hello, Jesus: The Religion of Martha and the Working Church

It is not an exaggeration to say that had the Church listened to Meister Eckhart instead of condemning him, the Church in which I grew up would have been entirely different. His sermons—many of which went underground because of their censure by the Inquisition—proved pivotal in the transition from the medieval to the modern world. He was one of the formative geniuses of the German language, whose German sermons translated medieval Latin theology into a vivid vernacular understandable to laypeople. He helped shift the attention of theology from otherworldly concerns to this world, to everyday life, and contributed to the cultivation of a mysticism of this world, what I am calling a religion of the rose. He anticipated much of the renewal that was called for in the Reformation but was crushed within Roman Catholicism itself by its counter-Reformation. That is the Catholicism that my generation inherited. Nobody ever brought up Meister Eckhart in the Council-of-Trent Catholicism in which I was brought up. His memory was lost to the Church until the end of the nineteenth century.

What I took away from Eckhart when I came upon him as a student is that the world is the place where God, or as I prefer to put it now, what is *going on in* the name of God is brought to bear, in fact and deed. Eckhart went so far as to say that God needs human beings in order to be God. This is the mystical predecessor of what I am calling the "insistence of God," where God needs us to be provided with existence. I am slowly building up the nerve to blurt out what I really think: that the world is the place where God gets to be God. Maybe if I put off saying that until the very end, I can get it out and then beat a hasty retreat before the Inquisition even learns my name. Maybe I should use a pseudonym to say it for me.

Eckhart opened up a new world for the Church, one that would have allowed Catholicism to enter the modern world willingly, instead of kicking and screaming in reaction to the Reformation and the birth of modern science, which is the sorry show it in fact put on.[1] Of course, that makes us appreciate Pope

Francis all the more—his 2015 encyclical on climate control[2] and poverty could actually forge an alliance of science and the Catholic Church, while so much of Protestantism sinks into climate change and science denial! But historically, Protestantism kept pace with the spirit of modernity, and Catholicism could have done the same. Either way, Eckhart's sermons were fraught with historical importance and ended up going to a place that Eckhart himself would not have approved. The kingdom of God is not up ahead; it is *here*, he preached. The kingdom of God is not the reward for the works of love and mercy. These works *are* the kingdom of God, here on earth. Housekeeping, cooking and cleaning, tending to the needs of the body, animal needs, the needs of the flesh, the most quotidian affairs of mundane life, let's say, the working church figured by Martha, are not means to an end— they are the unfolding life of God in the world. This contrasts sharply with the Neoplatonic version of Christianity, where we will have no more need of these lowly things when we shed our corporeality for incorporeal maintenance-free bodies in eternity.

The otherwise puzzling expression "secular theology" means that the secular order is not a neutral and transient means to a religious end. The secular order is the realization of the kingdom of God. This is a two-way street. It means both that theology is realized in secular structures and that secular structures can be traced back to an implicit theology. The body is not a drag on implementing the kingdom of God; it is the scene of its accomplishment. This more radical interpretation of the kingdom of God, which shows up in the theology of Paul Tillich and the later secular theologies, owes a long footnote to Eckhart's retelling of the story of Mary and Martha, even if Eckhart would have balked at these twentieth-century movements.

The divine quality of even the most quotidian things is released at the very moment they cease being a means to an end, at the very instant in which they are greeted without why and hailed as full of grace. But this quality is suppressed so long as temporal things are seen as a step on a ladder of ascent to eternity. Eckhart, and more recently Marguerite, supply the move I need to get beyond the constraints of the classical orthodoxy that once gave my life form and definition. Might there be something to Jackie's secret musings? What is the secret of the stars? A big Why in the Sky called God? Or do the stars tell us that our being-in-the-world is the unfolding life of God in the world?

It is not an accident that Eckhart invokes a biblical story of hospitality. Martha is preparing the house for the arrival of Jesus, which is a mystical figure for receiving God into the soul. The work that embodies the kingdom of God is a literal work of welcoming God into her house, her soul, her life. The religion of Martha is a religion of hospitality; it is not the means to attain the kingdom of God but its actualization. Hospitality and the gift are what they are if and only if they are offered unconditionally, that is, not performed for the sake of attaining the kingdom of God but as realizing it. Without them, we are left with Eckhart's Mary, what Hegel called a "beautiful soul," too beautiful to tarnish itself with hard work and housekeeping! When I am called before the Inquisition and told to please explain what madness made me rework the religion of my childhood and end up saying such outrageous things, I will blame it all on the rose. I will say I was sniffing something, stoned on the rose, on the unconditionality of a rose emitting an intoxicating aroma. I was not in my right mind. The rose made me do it. I will set before them the analysis of the unconditional gift, to which I will join the analysis of unconditional hospitality. They are all the evidence I have; then I will rest my case, so help me God.

Hospitality

In one of my lives, my professional life, where they call me "Dr." and "Professor," I am known as a "philosopher of religion." That has been my public persona for so long that even I sometimes believe it, although Jackie greets it with a hearty laugh every night. There is no fooling him, and he and I both know it. In my public career, I have made a profitable living off linking the "postmodern" with the biblical religious tradition. Part of my scholarly work has been bent on showing that a great deal of what is going on in postmodernism, in what is called *theory*—a blend of philosophy, literature, politics, and often psychoanalysis—can be traced back to the ancient biblical virtue of hospitality. What has particularly caught the eye of contemporary theorists—starting with the other Jackie—is nothing other than the distinction between conditional and unconditional hospitality.

In conditional hospitality, we practice hospitality "by invitation only," which is a harsh, most inhospitable and exclusionary phrase. Here we have the initiative and we extend an invitation whose terms we get to decide in advance. We welcome those we have chosen in advance, so that the offer is inevitably conditioned by a lot of ulterior motives. But in unconditional hospitality, we have lost the initiative. This is not an invitation we initiate but a visitation we did not see coming, which means that something visits itself upon us, requiring an unprepared, unconditional welcome, in a kind of naked exposure to the coming of the other.

I will stick close to the ground of two completely common-place examples, practices familiar to any churchgoer—because the Kingdom is something familiar and quotidian. But I warn you in advance. Do not be misled by the familiar examples, as I have something more sweeping and unfamiliar up my sleeve. I am all along building up to a somewhat nervy and unfamiliar account of God, luring my readers into doing a bit of "radical theology" while trying not to use or overuse that phrase or frighten them away. If I succeed, they will not know what hit them. But remember, these practices, gift-giving and hospitality, are not *applications* or *illustrations* of my theology; the radical part is that they *are* my theology. But I am getting ahead of myself again and tipping my hand. In a theology of the event, you are not supposed to see what is coming.[3]

Welcoming Congregations

If you have ever seen the expression "A Welcoming Congregation" posted on a church marquee as you drive by, you may know that this is code for saying these congregations welcome LGBTQ persons. Welcoming here does not mean welcoming sinners, loving the sinner but not the sin, which is better than hating both of them, but it is still duplicitous. It does not mean these congregations have a higher "tolerance" of this kind of aberration, or, God forbid, that they want to help them pray the gay away. It means they welcome LGBTQs in all their polyvalence as so many expressions of the polychromatic love of God. It means that they do not consider this sexual diversity to be depraved or deviant but an expression of the many ways that love multiplies and diffuses itself in the world, one of many houses in God's mansion. To say this is love's diffusion, not depravity, is to reaffirm a medieval formula, *bonum diffusivum sui*, the good diffuses and multiplies itself in multiple ways, or more loosely translated, the good goes viral, but all for the better. Even further back, Bernard of Clairvaux said that the only measure of love is love without measure. Love does not abide conditions; it does not come in proportioned measures and regulated doses (which is the very reason unconditional things like love are also very dangerous and permit the worst things to be done in their name). If you ask the love of your life point blank, "Do you love me?," and the beloved answers after a long and awkward pause, well, yes, under certain conditions, then, my friend, you're in trouble.

Jesus got himself into a barrel of trouble by associating with the outsiders, with prostitutes and tax-collectors (by which the Gospels meant Jewish collaborators with the Roman occupation, not respectable government employees). As one scholar has pointed out, the text says he associated with sinners, not "reformed" sinners.[4] The image of Jesus in the Gospels is of someone who systematically takes the side of the outliers, the lost sheep, the lost son, the lost coin, the woman taken in adultery; he was pushing the envelope, deconstructing the tables in the Temple. That is why we progressive types, like everyone else, cannot resist concluding that Jesus would be on our side today, that he would be just the sort of person who today would defend the role of women and the rights of same-sex love, just the sort who would incur the wrath of the Christian Right. I contend that if the Christian Right ever thought it through with any historical sensitivity, the last thing its dues-paying members would want is to do what Jesus would do. Indeed there is a delicious irony in the fact that the slogan of the Christian Right,

"What Would Jesus Do?," was a herald of the Social Gospel movement.[5] If a fellow like Jesus moved into their lily-white suburbs, the Christian Right would all move out.

When I am invited to speak by various church groups, I sometimes find myself preaching to the converted, to people who are already doing what I am theorizing, so that the most I can do for them is provide them with a vocabulary they can use at cocktail parties. The word "welcoming" these congregations have embraced is a hot topic in postmodern theory, but I find that the people on the ground, in the working church, are already *doing* what we theorists are theorizing. "Welcome," well-come, *bienvenu*, means to affirm the good (*bonum*) of the coming (*venire*) of the other. Welcome means the well-coming of the other, but in fact we usually welcome the same, those we have invited, while asking the invitees to be discreet about this invitation and not to bring it up in front of the others who were not invited. Welcoming too often comes down to welcoming the same and excluding the other, who are precisely not welcome.

It means issuing an invitation under a set of conditions we set in advance. When we say, "Make yourself at home," we would be outraged if our guests took us at our word and really did that. We invite the people we like, and try not to invite people we don't like. Sometimes what we call hospitality means inviting disagreeable relatives because it would be more trouble than it is worth not to invite them. Or people whose favor we are cultivating. Or we are returning an invitation (all part of the economy of exchange). In short, we welcome the same while carefully excluding the other.

A more radical welcome would be unconditional. It would be risky business, not an invitation we issue but an unforeseen *visitation*, requiring an *unconditional* openness to the other that puts itself at risk. A "welcoming community" is an idea that is under a lot of internal pressure. A "community" literally means a fort fortified (*munire*, as in munitions and ammunition) on every side, all around (*com*), with guns pointing in every direction *against* the coming of the other. A "welcoming community" is etymologically a puzzling notion, as is "hospitality," which is likewise made possible by sustaining an interior contradiction: welcoming the "*hostis*," a stranger who may be a guest in need of a "host" or who may be someone "hostile" (same word!) who may do you harm. If you remove the risk, you remove the teeth of the hospitality. That is why the other Jackie (Derrida) coined the word "hosti-pitality." My contention is that the tensions in the concept of hospitality are the very contradictions called for by the kingdom of God, where the first are last and the outsiders are in, a wedding feast where the guests are casual passersby, a kingdom of sinners, the ill-born and highly unroyal nothings and nobodies of the world (1 Corinthians 1).

The kingdom of God that Jesus describes in the Sermon on the Mount is arguably the most audacious document any of us will ever read. It is a perfect scandal to the good sense of the world and the centerpiece of the religion modeled after the mysticism of the rose, just because it calls for unconditional hospitality, returning those who hate you with love, and those who offend you with forgiveness. Offering love not to those who love us back but who do not, forgiving not those who beg our forgiveness and make amends (the "conditions" of forgiveness), but those who get in our face—loving and forgiving without conditions, without anything up our sleeve, without why.

There are church communities that engage in the most exclusionary excommunicative wagon-circling self-protective doctrine-driven undertakings. But the welcoming congregations are the radicals in the churches who defy the powers-that-be. They are blessing same-sex marriages, ordaining gays and lesbians, ordaining women to the priesthood and bishopric and making every effort to provide for women and homosexuals in the church, including on the faculties of seminaries and divinity schools. They are open-ended communities, communities without community, who welcome everyone. "Here comes Everybody," James Joyce said. Even the so-called "atheists" are welcomed aboard. I put this word in scare quotes because "atheism" has to do with a "belief," not with the deeper structure of faith and hope and love whose wares I am peddling under the name of the mysticism of the rose.

Hospitality, the heart of the most avant-garde and contemporary theory of the other, is the ancient virtue of desert travelers whose life depended upon being welcomed at the various stops along the way. In the story of the good Samaritan, the Samaritan is the placeholder for the other. The "other" is the one who hails from another part of town, or of the country, or of the world, of another color, gender, ethnic origin, religious belief, or no religious belief. The other comes in peace (or maybe not), which is why the mysticism of the rose is risky business, more like Martha than like Mary.

People who push the envelope in the "welcoming" congregations, people who make peace and serve the poor, the people in the working church, are the people on the ground in the kingdom of God, with or without God. They are the people of God, in the most radical, literal, material, and embodied sense, people who transform God's insistence into existence and give God a good name. They are the way God acquires mass and body. They are what God does, what God means, what is getting itself done in and under the name "God." That's my main idea, the idea to which I am trying to lead Jackie and Brother Paul, unless it is they who are leading me.

Inter-Faith Dialogue

The next concrete work of hospitality I choose is found in inter-faith dialogues that take place in the working church, when diverse communities of faith enter into dialogue in hope of reaching deeper understanding of their similarities and differences. Again, there are two ways to conduct these dialogues, the conditional way and the unconditional way. The conditional way keeps our own presuppositions safe; the unconditional way puts them at risk. The safe way says, I am not entering this dialogue except under certain conditions, that is, from the standpoint of my faith, which is strong. I would not expect you to respect me if I did not, and I expect you to do the same. I am prepared to put my presuppositions at risk, but only up to a certain point, where I draw the line. I will see just how far I can go before the ice starts to look a little thin and I am forced to turn back. So let's see where there is overlapping agreement between us; then, after seeing where we agree, let's shake hands and agree to disagree. Let's have a drink together after the meeting is over, just before we hit the road to return to our respective corners in the faith community from which we came, and agree not to launch another religious war.

That is commendable. If everyone did that, there would be no religious violence in the headlines and we would all be better off. I am not trying to put a stop to that. God forbid. I am just saying that it is as much intra-faith monologue as inter-faith dialogue, a bit more risk-free than risky, a bit more concerned with maintaining intra-faith composure than inter-faith exposure. It starts out by stating the conditions under which it is willing to extend a welcome to the other. It is trying to find out how much there is of the same in the other and trying to resonate in unison with the other. It is a conditional open-endedness that can end up saying what Karl Rahner said when he described those in good faith in other faiths as "anonymous Christians."[6] It is inclusive, trying to widen the circle to include the other in the space of the same, but without allowing that space to be altered. It sees the other as an anonymous version of the same.

Karl Rahner was one of the heroes of my Catholic youth, although I am closer intellectually to Hans Küng, his fellow Jesuit who was the real hero of Vatican II. Rahner, who was an earnest man and in good faith, was perfectly willing to reverse the formula, willing to say that Jesuits are anonymous Buddhists. But you can only get so far with this model; it's the model that is at fault, not the good will of a brilliant theologian like Rahner. (Women are anonymous men; non-Westerners are anonymous Westerners, etc.) What is wrong is the presupposition about religious truth: the parties to the dialogue assume the coherence of the idea of "the true religion," meaning that one religion is true at the expense of another, in a zero-sum game, where the best we can do is find some overlapping consensus and then agree to disagree. That I reject all the way down, or from the bottom up.

We need another model, one a good deal riskier, one that starts out with a simple but unnerving point. When I was lecturing once in the Middle East, I met a Muslim theologian who was born and has spent his entire life in the Middle East, who had no hesitation in pointing out to me after my talk that were we switched at birth, I would be the Muslim and he would be the American Catholic from southwest Philadelphia. Religion cannot be detached from its cultural context. Mathematics can be, but religion cannot. If we were switched at birth and learned mathematics in Mozambique instead of Massachusetts, the mathematical proofs and truths would be the same. While the interests of the mathematicians might differ from place to place, mathematical truths are what they are. The principles do not depend on where we were born, or when, or upon our gender, race, ethnicity, or whether we are hatless or wearing a turban or a baseball cap while we work on them. But religion is a form of life and so it is like hats—clothing, language, music, food and culture—not like mathematics. Religion is very much a matter of where we were born and when.

That's what the faithful like to call "amazing grace." But a more neutral observer would call it a not very amazing, highly probable, and statistically predictable feature of an accident of birth. Save the idea of grace for something more amazing than that. It would be much more amazing if this fellow grew up a Catholic and I a Muslim. Switched at birth, everything that is in my head and baked into my bones would be inside his, and vice versa. Switched-at-birth stories in literature, like Mark Twain's *Puddin'head Wilson*, are diving into deep theological as well as social and political waters. Each culture represents a different way to sing a song to the world. Religion is more like a turban than a triangle.

Otherwise a "divine revelation" ends up being dependent upon an accident of birth and salvation is a lottery in which you don't even get to buy the ticket yourself. You just wake up one day, as I did, in Jackie's world, with a ticket already in your hand (your "Godparents" stood in line for you and bought the ticket). Everybody speaks English, the house is full of crucifixes and pictures of the baby Jesus, the whole family and everyone you meet is Italian Catholic, and they all pray to Jesus to help Philadelphia sports teams have a winning season. The "gift of faith" would then turn out to mean you just happened to be standing in the right place at the right time when the divine motorcade went speeding by and you saw your redeemer.

Ideas like the "chosen people" or a "special revelation" make everything worse, unless you can find some delicate way to walk them back. For example, the Jewish philosopher Emmanuel Levinas says we are *all* chosen, that instead of a great privilege given to the people God chose above all others, we are all put in the accusative by the coming of the other who lays claim to us without being invited.[7] We are all guilty, Dostoevsky says, but I more than others. Levinas loved the Torah more than God. He was not interested in God as a Supreme Being looming behind the scenes but in what is going on in the name (of) "God," the call that insists in this name, here and now, in space and time, which does not play favorites—it accuses everyone! By the same token, in a more hospitable accounting of revelation, every revelation is a special revelation. You don't have to be born in the right place at the right time to receive a revelation. You just have to be born, period; in a culture, period; and the revelation comes along in the package, period. A culture is a package deal, no à la carte items. Every culture has a revelation; every revelation requires a culture. Everyone has a revelation, or else they would be dead or never born.

Everybody's revelation is "special," just the way everybody's spouse or child or family or hometown is special. Speaking of a "special revelation" packs the same punch as the praise we heap on our parents at their fiftieth wedding anniversary where by unanimous consent and to much applause and raised glasses we proudly proclaim them the best parents in the world. Each disclosure is a distinct way the world is opened up, a unique form of life uniquely embedded in a language and a culture and baked into the bones of the people born there. That is, unless you have been very badly placed in that culture, if you are born poor and disadvantaged, making you a very badly displaced person, which in this unjust world of ours happens all the time. That's the thorn in the rose, the time when smiles turn to tears. Of course, people do relocate or adopt a new religion, but that is like learning a foreign language; it takes years of immersion and happens infrequently, and you never really shed the parent culture built into your bones. There are multiple forms of life and they are all special, but no one has any special privileges. Special really means the local species. To treat it as privileged is to court religious violence. We are always already embedded in concrete cultures and their revelations, while also remaining structurally exposed to the unconditional, to the coming of the other, to the chance of being-otherwise were we born in some other place and time.

I cannot resist adding, only half in jest, that the implausibility of the classical idea of a special revelation, and my extreme postmodern incredulity toward it, would slacken slightly if for once, just *once*, there were an instance in all of recorded history when one of its advocates would say, "There is indeed a special revelation, the one true one, but I regret to report that we have lost the lottery. Our application to host the theological Olympics has been rejected. The Messiah has come—but not to us! The Messiah was given to the others and we were passed over! We are the *un*chosen people. *We* were the ones left out!" That brings up another difference between religion and mathematics: people readily recognize that when it comes to the gift of mathematical brilliance they got the short end of the stick; but somehow they always inherit the true religion, the big stick. That would be very funny were it not so dangerous.

Faith without Beliefs, Hope without Assurance

What I have been saying about welcoming congregations and inter-faith dialogue is part of a more general point that, after conducting an extended review, I cannot find discussed in my faded dog-eared copy of the Baltimore Catechism. This point concerns a more elusive faith and hope at work in the working church but nowhere to be found in the Little Church.

An unconditional inter-faith dialogue, one that has some teeth, starts with what Heidegger called our "thrownness" into the world. That word flourished back in my college days, in the heyday of "Existentialism," and we used it all the time. Jean-Paul Sartre, the most popular philosopher in the world in those days, got a lot of mileage out it. It was avant-garde in those days to be "thrown"; being "born" was very retrograde. Thankfully, Hannah Arendt and the feminists descended on that and eventually rehabilitated beautiful words like *birth* and *natality*. We find ourselves "thrown" into the place where we wake up in the world.[8] One of the Kierkegaardian pseudonyms captured the whole point of thrownness with the quip, "Why was I not asked about it? . . . Is there no manager? To whom shall I make my complaint?" (about being born in the first place).[9] The meaning of "faith" in the conditional form of "inter-faith" takes place entirely on the level of beliefs. Beliefs are the things that get inside our head in virtue of an accident of birth. They are part of our inherited religious identity, making up the various creeds or creedal "confessions." Beliefs are the positions we inherit from our parents or our culture and they can be given the form of propositions to which fellow believers all nod in consent. Beliefs are the sort of thing that switches on at birth, and that switches on differently if you are switched at birth. In short, beliefs belong to the religion of the Little Church.

Belief is to be distinguished from faith as the conditional from the unconditional. We can unplug from a religious belief altogether or try to convert to another. We can weaken our cultural or religious identity, learn another language, relocate. But faith is a more underlying matter from which we cannot or at least ought not unplug. Faith has to do with a deeper fidelity, a deeper responsibility to what is calling upon or visiting itself upon us unconditionally, wherever we live and whatever we believe. When beliefs deepen, entrenchment sets in, fundamentalism waxes, searching wanes. When faith deepens, beliefs are destabilized, searching waxes, fundamentalism wanes. This deeper faith goes hand in hand with a more deeply lodged hope in the promise, in what is to-come, which lacks assurances about the object of our hope. Instead of inter-faith meetings—which run the risk of being trade fairs in which we browse the aisles of the beliefs of others—I prefer "inter-hope" dialogues, in which we share our dreams and hopes in an effort to encourage one another. Faith and hope on the level of the unconditional are much riskier things—more "unprotected," as in unprotected sex. Faith cannot fall back on millennia-old traditions, ancient manuscripts, Gothic cathedrals, liturgies, and prayer books, along with all the incense and candles you want to back them up. Faith arises from a more obscure and distant call, an ambiguous solicitation, and a hope in an uncertain future. It demands that we assume responsibility for a past we had nothing to do with shaping and a hope for a future we cannot control, while admitting that we have not been hard-wired in advance to The Truth.

I hasten to cut off a possible confusion. I am not saying that once we get past these culturally different empirical belief systems we will come upon a deeper faith that is the same across all cultures. I am not advancing the claim of the old comparative religion theory of a generation ago. I do not think that there is an underlying, universal, cross-cultural religious truth that can finally be unearthed with enough empirical digging into the different traditions. The only universal I embrace is the universality of difference. I do not advance the idea that if you dig deep enough into the different you will hit the core of the same. That is the *last* thing I mean. I just got done saying that each form of life is unique, different, special but not privileged. Its only privilege is that it is *mine*, but that comes with a massive proviso: were I born there, there would be here. The unconditional is not an essence or a universal. It has to do with promises and hopes, recollections of things that have never been, hopes for things that will never be, things of which we dream, for which we pray and weep. Such things are as varied as the songs we sing, the languages we speak, the poems we write, the music we play, the stories we tell, which are as deep as any treatise by Aristotle. These differing cultural forms of life are irreducibly diverse, unforeseeably surprising. Nothing says that underneath they are all the same.

As opposed to the zero-sum idea of "belief" in the "one true religion," I borrow an image from the late Nelson Mandela: a "rainbow" model of religious truth, a polymorphic, polyvalent, polychromatic plurality of forms of life, each of which bows before the coming of the "other." I imagine a meeting of Jesus and the Buddha, in which each bows before the other, each confessing what he has to learn from the other, a scene that won't play well in Alabama. I resist the idea that if we dig deep enough we will find that everybody turns out to be the same as resolutely as I resist the idea that there is only one true form of life. There is not one true blue form of life but a rainbow; and while it is true, it is not The Truth.[10] It is one of many truths. Let there be as many different ways to be true as possible; as many ways to smile, to sing the world. Let the rose blossom as it will and let there be as many different kinds of rose as possible. I am not talking about so many isolated islands in an archipelago, each one curled up in a circle of self-identity. I mean a community without community, open-ended networks of interrelated mortals, an inter-faith gathering of non-knowers, each of whom begins by confessing that we are all in this together. That also means that we are all equally lost, all in need of guidance, because we do not know who we are, where helping one another is the blind leading the blind.

The important thing to see here is that the unconditional is not the one common essence-of-religion that unites us all, the way human beings all have lungs and kidneys. Religion is not like having lungs, it is like having a language; it is not like having hair on your head, it is more like wearing a hat. There are fundamentally different assumptions about time and becoming in the Buddhist and Christian thinking and nothing is gained by trying to reduce all "religions" (which is already a reductionistic word) to being at bottom the same. Of course, we could certainly find some overlapping similarities, maybe some version of the golden rule, in just the way the prohibition of incest is a common feature of profoundly different cultures. Nor is it even enough to say we each have our own identity. What's truly interesting is that we are not even identical with ourselves, that we are all inhabited from within by the other. There are many voices within us, many genders, many races, many stories, too many to count or comprehend, and they give each other no rest. This has always been true, but nowadays its truth has been intensified to a fever pitch, now that we can travel anywhere (if we can afford the fare), or have anything we are interested in come to us in virtual space (if we can afford the technology). In the postmodern world of advanced transportation and information technologies, the multiplex and multicultural diversity of life now comes rushing in upon us, inundating us in waves of differences. We postmodern people are becoming less and less identical with ourselves, and more rapidly so with each passing day.

In saying this I think in particular of the personal story of the other Jackie, Jacques Derrida, the leading luminary of the postmodern theory of welcoming and the gift, who I think of as a model of the unconditional idea of faith and of inter-faith that I am advocating. Derrida was a *pied noir*, a French-speaking Algerian, born in 1930 into a middle-class Jewish family, in colonial Algeria, a country dominated by the Franco-Catholic culture of the occupiers. He said of himself that he had only one language, but it was not his own. By this he did not mean that he had no first or native language, but that his native language was not his. Born into an Arab country, he might have spoken Arabic or Berber. Born into a Jewish family, he might have spoken Hebrew, but he only learned enough Hebrew to get past Bar-Mitzvah. Instead, he spoke what he called "Christian Latin French," the language of "*les Catholiques*," which showed up in the practice of the Algerian Jews speaking of "circumcision," in Christian Latin, instead of the Hebrew *brit milah* (Yiddish, *Bris*). Every time he opened his mouth he spoke the language of the other. After growing up in Algeria, he migrated to France, tried to suppress his Algerian accent and speak pure Parisian French, and then became even more famous in the United States than back home in France, where he always remained something of an outsider to the academic establishment. Traveling the world incessantly, he claimed that he was always being made welcome "elsewhere." His patron saint, if he had ever felt the need for one, would have been *St. Elsewhere*, to recall a superb American television series from the 1980s.

Derrida once said of himself that he "rightly passed for an atheist."[11] When asked, why he did not say I *am* an atheist, he said it was because he did not know if he were. That is what people say of him and, by the standards of the local rabbi, that is correct. But the deeper truth (beyond correctness) and deeper faith (beyond belief) is that there are many voices inside him, and they give each other no rest, so that he cannot say who or what he is, as if that were something final or finished. *Atheist* and *theist* have to do with beliefs, positions that condense into propositions meant to represent entities, which are contingent and even birth-switchable. The truth has to do with a deeper and more ambiguous faith and hope. His "rightly passing for" provides a splendid formula for theology, for any deeper faith in the unconditional. What better way to describe the nature of the hold we have on any belief we think we hold, for any contingent opinion we have formed based on the shifting times and tides of circumstance and accidents of birth? Do we not all "rightly pass" for something or other, for Christian or Muslim, theist or atheist, right-wingers or left-wingers, "or whatever," as we say in our postmodern age—while more deeply considered we are all a great question to ourselves? Derrida's remark parallels a famous saying by Johannes Climacus, one of Kierkegaard's most important pseudonyms, who declined to claim he was a Christian and said instead that he was "trying to become" one.

In sum, and this is what I cannot find in my catechism, the more unconditional model of hospitality is the rule without rule that reigns in the kingdom of God. The Kingdom is made up of beings of a deeper darker faith communicating in a midnight rendezvous, whatever they may "rightly pass for" during daylight hours. This darker dialogue takes place among communities of faith, communities of those without community practicing an unconditional faith, a faith without protection from doubt. Such people dare to let their beliefs weaken in order to allow a more underlying but unstable faith break through and to permit the appearance of a more elementary hope in a more indelible but indiscernible promise. The rose blossoms among communities of non-knowers, gathered in the night of non-knowing, among those who cannot see what is coming. There a smile breaks out on the surface of matter, a rose blossoms unseen in a remote corner of infinity, and then all too soon is gone. The cosmos—that vaunting arch that Jackie has been contemplating these many years—moves on, en route to the absolutely unthought. About this religion, the priests and nuns kept their counsel.

So therefore let us pray to God that we may be free of "God."
—Meister Eckhart[1]

CHAPTER SIX

Adieu to God: Praying God to Rid Us of God

I remember once that Brother Paul, fearful that he could no longer endure the discipline of the Novitiate—the thirteenth century can be tough!—and worried that he was going to "defect," the word we used for "losing" our vocation, thought that maybe he would be lucky and something would happen to him and he would die before he gave in. That was just a bad day, of course, and as the director of novices used to say about spiritual trials, "this too will pass." Still, it is instructive. Brother Paul was only eighteen years old at the time. The one thing the priests and nuns had convinced me of when I was growing up is that I should bend all my efforts to "saving my soul" and that it was foolish in the extreme, completely shortsighted, to pursue the goods of this life in time at the expense of eternal life. That sound economics, I thought, was to be the bottom line, the one non-negotiable, in whatever I was going to do for the next sixty or seventy years or so, which seemed like small potatoes compared to life everlasting. Holy Mother the Church is the one safe refuge from a world that will try to convince me otherwise.

That thought sustained me—until it did not. Under the influence of philosophy and other corrupting forces that I encountered in the world beyond the popes and priests and nuns of my childhood, and after the deeper meditations that Brother Paul and I conducted upon these matters, I have concluded otherwise. The absolute and unshakeable truth that I once thought was baked into my bones proceeds from a corrupted idea of time and the body—and of God. Thinking in terms of the economy of salvation distorts the gift of God. That, I now think, is how *not* to think of God. How, then, to speak of God? I can no longer dance around this question. The time has come to speak out.

I had decided to leave the De LaSalle Brothers to pursue the life of a philosopher. But as it turned out, my religious life followed me out the door and pursued me the rest of my life, unless it was I who pursued it. Either way, my life as a philosophy professor has taken place in the distance between theology and philosophy. Like everyone else, however far forward I thought I had moved, I was always circling around my origins. I soon found that the audacity of the philosophers who "dare to think," according to the Enlightenment motto, fails them when it comes to theology. There they panic, in fear of contamination. They treat the name of God like a terrible computer virus that will corrupt all their files, or like a real one, like the Ebola virus, where the odds of recovering are against you. So, mostly at the beginning of my professorial life, when "John D." stepped forth and responded to the title "professor," while telling Jackie to stay at home, I was worried that they would say, "This is not philosophy; this is just his religion." But my religion is between me and Brother Paul and Jackie and several others. How could they know anything about that?

Later on, after my tongue was loosened by the other Jackie, I simply relented. I gave up the pretense that we can police these borders, that philosophy could or should be kept "pure" of theology or that theology should or could be purified of philosophy.[2] Instead of fearing contamination, I embraced cross-pollination, creative cross-breeds, and innovative hybrids. So I came out of the closet. That is how it was put by Catherine Keller, a kindred theological spirit in so many ways for me, writing a blurb for *The Weakness of God*, who said that in this book I came out of the closet as a theologian. It is disconcerting to see one's whole life contracted into a blurb. Is "theology" an accusation against which I should vigorously protest or a congratulation that modesty prevents me from accepting? Should I deny that I have anything to do with theology and then, like Peter, hear the cock crow three times? Or should I humbly confess that I have never gotten as far as theology? It all comes down to God. All my life long, from my earliest recollections—I can remember the day that F.D.R. died—to the so-called golden years, it will have turned out I have been asking, How is it possible to speak of God? But then again, how is it possible *not* to? What to say, or not-say, of God?

In this chapter I will set out the conceptual heart of the book, the core idea I have about God that I have been leading up to all along by analyzing various cases of the unconditional. I will present the view that the proper way to speak of God is to say not that God exists, but that God insists, while we are called upon to make up the difference. We are asked to pick up where God leaves off, to fill up the existence that is lacking in the insistence of God. God insists, but the weight of God's existence falls on us. The easy yoke and incredible lightness of God's insistence implies that the gravity of existence is our responsibility, that the burden of existence falls on our shoulders. As the mystics say, God needs us.

The Evidence of the Rose

I spent my earliest years having as little to do with books as I could get away with and as much time as I was allowed on the city streets playing cards and baseball. If I am reincarnated I would like to come back as a bookish child who is taunted by the other kids. I would have thick eyeglasses earned at an early age from too much reading, having started on my own the study of Sanskrit at the age of six—instead of memorizing baseball statistics. I would go on to a career as a biblical archeologist, my life's work being dedicated to unearthing a lost fragment of the book of Exodus in which Yahweh says to Moses, "I am not who I am. I am certainly not who you think I am. I am wholly otherwise than you expect." It would be perfect if this fragment continued to say, "I live like the rose, without why," but I must be realistic in my expectations, even in a reincarnation.

In the absence of discovering an authoritative, inerrant text to back me up, or of the election of a pope who could come to my aid by just declaring my views infallible, I fall back on the only evidence I have, the sole evidence of the rose. All the phenomena that I have presented up to now, the gift and hospitality, forgiveness and works of mercy, love and compassion, point in the same direction. Wherever we turn, the results are the same: these bountiful and beautiful works are what they are in virtue of their unconditionality. Only when a gift is given unconditionally, without the expectation of a return, is the gift what it is. Only when hospitality is offered unconditionally, without dividing the invited from the uninvited, is hospitality what it is. So too with love and forgiveness. The conclusion is inescapable, try as I might to flee from it, it pursues me down every corridor. The name of God, of the God who is love, of the God who is the giver of all good gifts, is the name of the unconditional. God loves, gives, and forgives unconditionally, without why, nothing hidden up the divine sleeve (where there would be plenty of room, infinite room, to keep things concealed).

Does this mean I am trying to come up with another proof for the existence of God? Does it not follow inescapably? God is the unconditional ground of all good gifts and of everything unconditional. Ergo, God is The Unconditional, capitalized and in the singular. You see the problem. We are back in the business of religion, the old theological business, the big business of large-cap Big Being omnipotence theology. We are back in a theology of The One with all the power to reward and punish. This One you anger at your peril. A so-called wisdom begins in fearing Him (sic!), and if you ask Him (sic!) too many questions he will get red in the face and shout you down with a mighty voice demanding to know where you were when He (sic!) laid the foundations of the earth. Better to keep your counsel in the face of that. My apologies, of That.

Mercifully, we have been saying the unconditional does not exist. That solves that problem. Thank God, but don't tell my nuns. But here I must proceed with caution because I am not saying there is nothing to God. I am only saying that the unconditional is not a Big Being or a Super Being. I have put all my chips on this: the pure gift, pure hospitality, do not exist. What does exist occupies the conditioned, contextual space of concrete reality, so that whatever happens, happens in the space between the unconditional and the conditional. If I have come up with a proof of anything, and I am not saying I have, it is not of the existence of God but of God's inexistence! The unconditional solicits us and we respond, and what exists, exists in response to the call. The unconditional insists; we exist. The call of and for love and forgiveness and mercy are all truly unconditional, but it is also true that they depend upon us to make all that come true. The unconditionals—in the plural and the lower case; these are all small-cap stocks— do not exist; they interrupt the conditions of existence. The conditioned exists but in continual unrest and exposure to what insists. This is where I have been driven, the point I have reached: if the unconditional does not exist, and if the name of God is the name of something unconditional, then God does not exist—just in virtue of the unconditional purity of the gift, of forgiveness, of everything unconditional. I would say *quod erat demonstrandum*, except I was not trying to demonstrate anything. I am praying and weeping over it and trying to be a worthy son of these tears.

While that solves the first problem, it creates a still more unsettling problem. If God does not exist, how can God be God? What good is God? What good can God do for us? How can we even *speak* of God? Then, again, how can we *not*? How can we *not-speak* of God, speak without speaking? If God does not exist, is that the end of it? Is there nothing to God, to the name of God?

Religion, thank God, is not God. Religion exists and so it falls on the side of the conditioned, not the unconditional. Indeed, as we have seen, it falls with quite a thud, bringing with it a plethora of conditions—of codes and creeds and institutional protocols and people with institutional authority. Left to its own devices, this whole business of religion would institutionalize the gift and enter the works of mercy and compassion into an economy, seeing to it that the good are properly rewarded and the not-so-good properly punished, up to the point of being eternally merciless with those who do not show mercy, and eternally unforgiving to those who do not forgive. Given a free hand, the business of religion is to regulate the unruliness of the gift and to contain the uncontainable excess that makes these mad and beautiful things what they are. I am not saying there is nothing good in religion. Remember what I said at the beginning, that after the cameras are gone, most of the people still around to aid the victims of a disaster are religious people. I am just saying that too often the good that is going on in religion has a tough time making it to the surface. My task here is to help religion out of the hole it keeps digging for itself.

So the conclusion I have reached is that religion's God is too large, too great, too Big a Why-in-the-Sky for things down here on earth to live without why. God is without why, but religion is chuck full of why's and wherefore's. The God of religion is too violent a whirlwind for the delicate petals of the gift. Such a God cannot be God. We need to get rid of such a God. Better still, since we are hardly up to such a task, we need God to rid God of God. Pursuing that line of reflection troubled my spirit greatly and I sought consolation from this tribulation. Surely, I thought, I am not alone in this. Surely someone else has observed this gaping abyss, this black hole that is sucking me into its bowels. Surely somewhere, someone has reported seeing it. Then I found it, or better I remembered it from the days of my monkish fascination with the mystics: "So therefore let us pray to God that we may be free of 'God.' " That is what I have been looking for. I can cite a master, chapter and verse. This is not my own concoction. I am doing nothing more than following the good counsel of the mystics, those insidious insiders who make such salutary trouble for religion. I take Meister Eckhart at his word that the highest prayer, the prayer of all prayers, is to pray God to rid us of God. Thank God for Meister Eckhart whose God is God only if God is rid of God.

Adieu to God (*adieu à Dieu*). Farewell to Religion's God, to the Master of the House, to the Lord High Governor and Supreme Administrator of the Economy of Salvation and Supreme Separator of Sheep and Goats (royals have long names and numerous titles). God save us from that God. I am not up to this myself. I am praying God to rid God of God but—and everything depends on grasping this—in the very same breath I am praying that God may be God in the world. I pray that the world may become the place where God, having abdicated his (sic) royal seat, may be God with us. The Inquisition will not stand for this, so if they ever catch up with me, God help me, I will blame it all on the Meister.

I put forth Meister Eckhart's saying not as the rock on which we build a new religion—God help us, we have enough religions already, history is full of them—but as the rose, the attar of rose, on whose aroma I have gotten stoned. To have a taste for the mystics requires having a nose for the rose, a nose for the unexpected. So if you expected religion to bring "good news," be prepared for the shocking headline in the first edition, that this religion is praying God to be rid of God if the work of God is to be done—as well as praying religion to be rid of religion, too: "I hate, I despise, your festivals, and I take no delight in your solemn assemblies," Amos has the Lord God say (Amos 5:21). God must be rid of God—in the name of the gift, in the name of hospitality. God must be rid of God—in the name of God. In a religion modeled after the humility and simplicity of the rose, we seek to live Marguerite's simple life and to cease all that boastful uppercase chest-thumping. We do not say that God is The Unconditional. Instead, in gentler tones, in a more peaceful and prayerful quiet, out in the desert like Jesus, we say that the name of God is the name of the unconditional. That means, not that God exists, but that what calls to us unconditionally—insistently, incessantly calling for peace and justice, for the gift and forgiveness, for mercy and hospitality—is called in and under the name of God. In short, God does not exist; God insists.

God is love and love is without why. What is done in and under the name of God is done for love. If God is love, creation is for free. For sheer love of the world, God declines to be the Final End that demeans every finite being into a means to an end, something to use but not enjoy, as Augustine enjoins. *Pace*

Augustine, if the gift of creation is truly a gift, then we are being told, "Take it. It's yours. Enjoy." God does not go out into creation in order to have creation returned to God, thereby undoing the whole thing. That's Neoplatonism, not Christianity. God goes out without return. God is not a celestial toll taker who charges a fee to undertake a spiritual journey. In short, God is not a Big Deal or Big Dealer, not the Omni-being who overwhelms our finitude with a plan to reward His (sic) friends and punish His enemies (sic, even sicker), which does not sound much like the Sermon on the Mount.

The time has come—in the name of God—to dim down the blazing glory of the divine countenance in order to let a smile appear on the surface of the world. The time has come to let God disappear into the world in order to allow the rose to blossom without why, off in a remote corner of the universe, unseen by anyone anywhere. In this rather unorthodox doxology, the glory of the divine countenance is deflected to the glory on the face of the world. That deflection bends religion back into the toils and troubles of everyday life, so that it is not merely the stuff of Sabbath rest. The mysticism of the rose is to be translated into the thorny practices of Martha's world, into the risky business of life, like giving without return and welcoming the stranger without condition. Religion is not merely the dreamy business of Mary's world, of hymns and candles and long robes with eyes directed unctuously toward another world. If God insists, but God does not exist, then there is no Big Being coming to save us, or to reward us, or to punish us. Living under the promptings of God we are asked to assume some responsibility for ourselves and realize that things are riskier than we expected.

None of which means that there is nothing to God.

If ever I have to face the Inquisition for having taken what it will no doubt judge a rash and imprudent position, given that I cannot afford a canon lawyer, my only recourse will be to present them with a rose. My entire case reposes upon the rose. My model in this regard is what Jesus would do. Jesus is my precedent for this foolishness. In the Legend of the Grand Inquisitor, Jesus, put in the same spot, turned away the wrath of the Lord Cardinal with a kiss. As I am not Jesus and I am not sure I could kiss a Cardinal, I would present him with a rose. Then I will try to save my skin by shamelessly blaming everything on the rose. I was seduced neither by a snake nor a woman but by sniffing a rose. If the Lord Cardinal demands a name, I will make one up. The name of the rose is Rosamond, which he will suspect is a pseudonym, no doubt. But I will insist; the name the rose gave me was Rosamond, unless, in my excitement I misheard. Maybe it was all in the Latin of my childhood. Maybe I heard *rosa munda*, meaning a rose pure and clean, or maybe even I heard *rosa mundi*, the rose of the world.[3] I was out of my senses at the time and it is hard to recall the scene. Then I will rest my case. God help me.

But that gives me another idea. If I get out of there alive, and if ever some fabulously wealthy and anonymous benefactor who shares with me a love of the mystics gives me the funding, I will start up a new religious order called the Order of the Saint Rosamond. We will be known as the Rosamondians and relying upon the intercession of our patron saint and founding spirit. Our mission will be to come to the aid of all dissidents, heretics, and other creative spirits who find themselves called before such an unforgiving court.

God Does Not Exist, God Insists

The shock delivered by the "good news" of the religion of the rose, I propose, is as follows:

> God does not exist.
> God insists.

God insists but dares not exist.[4] Everything I mean by God, and by hope, and by the God of hope, everything I mean when I speak of God flows from this. God insists *without* existence. God's inexistence is the condition of the existence of the rose. But everything I mean also depends upon realizing that this does not mean there is nothing to God. These two statements must be taken together. They should be read as one, as stating two sides of one statement—*God's insistence is God's inexistence.* That is the ground, or rather the groundless ground, of my idea of grace, which is the grace of the rose. If instead of a biblical archeologist, I were reincarnated as a prophet, this is the one claim I would have to a vision or a revelation, the thing chiseled on a stone tablet handed to me on a mountain by some stranger who would not give me his name. In exalting God in the highest, I am exalting the heights of inexistence, not the exalted super-existence traditionally attributed to God by the theologians of the supernatural. In proclaiming God's excess, existence is subtracted in order to add to God's insistence. To rid God of God is to rid God of existence in order to release God's insistence in all its unconditional purity. To rid God of God is to simplify God down to the purity of an unconditional call that calls upon and disturbs the conditions of the world, where we in turn are called to lead the simple life. That is my story, take it or leave it. God help me.

But, to be brutally honest, what good would insistence do if God is rid of existence? How would ridding God of existence contribute to a divine order? How can God be God if God is rid of existence? How can the kingdom of God be established if God is deprived of existence? Can a God like this be preached? What would they make of it out in the pews?

The answer is that God's inexistence is the *only* condition under which the work that is done in and under the name of God can be done. This is the only thing that can be preached—otherwise we're going to end up selling snake oil. God's inexistence is the condition under which the conditions of the world are transformed, shocked, and jolted by an excessive demand that seems positively unreal, like a pure gift, or pure hospitality, or pure forgiveness. The insistence of God means that the name of God is the name of something that lays claim to us unconditionally, like a promise of things that eye has not seen nor ears heard, but without the force of being, power, sovereignty, and omnipotence. It means that something calls upon us unconditionally, but without the power of an economic system of rewards or retributions or an army, even without a heavenly host of angels, to back it up.

Religion is supposed to subdue the forces of nihilism described by Lyotard. But I have been maintaining all along that a God all that almighty, such a Mighty Separator of Sheep and Goats, would wipe the smile off the face of the earth and crush underfoot the delicate grace of the rose that blossoms without why. In the religion modeled after the mysticism of the rose, God declines to be a party to the war on nihilism—precisely for God's sake, precisely to allow the work of God, *what is done in and under the name of God*, to take place, precisely in order to allow the grace of the rose to flourish. God is unconditional without force, something unconditional without sovereign power. To say God is insistent without existence is to say God calls, God solicits, God lures, God invites, but without the force of arms. God calls for justice, or mercy, or forgiveness, for a cup of cold water for the wayfarer—without compromise, without delay, here and now and always—without why.

The power of God has nothing to do with force, be it the force of omnipotence, or the force of an Inerrant Book or of an Infallible Pope, or of anything else that passes itself off as having Dropped From the Sky. The power of God is a powerless power, like the power of a kiss in face of wrath, the power of forgiveness instead of retaliation, like forgiving those who persecute you, loving those who hate you. This does not mean that God is the secret supernatural power that enables us to forgive; it means that forgiving is God's coming to be, that answering the call to forgive is how God comes to be God. God's power is that of a solicitation, but not the power to promise a reward or threaten a punishment, to make our enemies our footstool, which is the undoing of the gift. God's unconditional call for justice lifts God out of the conditions of existence, where things are always more or less unjust, promises more or less compromised, thereby keeping God pure of being and existence, even as in turn it exposes being and existence to the insistence of something unconditional. The world is made restless by God.

The insistence of God means that the name of God is the name of an unconditional visitation upon our lives that does not stand upon an invitation, that calls upon us with a weak force, without being able to force itself upon us. The powerless power of God is the power of forgiveness given without prior conditions, of gifts given without recompense. God lives like the rose, without why, without being the end-all and the be-all of a Final Reward or Punishment, without being an end at all but a beginning. God lives without being the end whom no one can see without dying, but by being a beginning, a synonym not for death but for giving birth. The name (of) "God" is the way we nominate a call that calls upon us *unconditionally but without force*, with unconditional love purified of power, unconditional hope purified of guarantees, all without why.[5] With or without God. That is the way the other Jackie would put it, or rather I would put it for him, or rather the way I would put it now having exposed Jackie to the other (Jackie) in a game of Jacks I cannot keep straight.

God's inexistence is not indifference; it does not mean merely to stand on the sidelines and watch helplessly as the world goes its unwieldy way. God's inexistence is risky business, not a calculated risk but a radical risk taken out of incalculable love for the world. Of all the mysteries that surround the *mysterium tremendum*, none is more tremendous than God's inexistence. Of all the hiddenness that engulfs the *deus absconditus*, none is more hidden than God's inexistence. Of all the love for the world God shows, none is deeper than God not thinking existence something to be seized upon and emptying the divine being into the world.[6]

The countenance of the Inquisitor is darkening, his brow is wrinkling. But I hold my ground. This much is clear. Whatever else it means, God's inexistence means that it is as much a mistake to simply affirm that God exists as it is to simply deny that God exists, the emphasis here falling on the "simply." When it comes to God, the debate between "theism" and "atheism" is a mistake, a *category* mistake—like arguing over whether you can steal third base in football—a mistake about the very terms in which what is going on in the name of God should be addressed, the very order to which it belongs. Thinking about God as a Supreme Being can lead to a militant theism, which is as wrongheaded as the warrior atheists we see today, who simply deny that any such Supreme Being exists and attack religion as simply irrational. Two opposing armies on the battlefields of existence aiming equally lethal weapons at each other. The one position is as militantly ham-fisted as the other, resulting in an argument that can be concluded only by the physical exhaustion of both sides, only with the "end of thought" at the time of the solar catastrophe! These combatants would continue to shout at each other from the grave, which is why they should not be buried in the same cemetery, lest they destroy the rest and peace of their neighbors.

The insistence of God means there is something to God, but that does not mean God exists. It means God insists, that something is going on in the name of God. It is not that there is a Supreme Being up there to reckon with—but that there is something going on. "There is," as we say in English, "*il y a*," in French, while the Germans say "*es gibt*," all to the same effect: something is going on there, not a being doing something, but something getting itself done there, in the middle voice, in the name.[7] There is something *to* the name of God, something going on *in* it. There is something being done *under* that name. This "there is," and what there is going on there—that is the one thing about the insistence of God upon which I insist. Except for the second thing, which is that this insistence happens, this being-called takes place. There is shocking news, and because there is, we must summon up the nerve to confront it. But what is there in this "there is" that merits our attention?

The good news is a shock, and the shock is this: God dares not to be. God takes the extreme risk, and nothing could be more extreme, of leaving being and existence in our hands. In ridding God of God, God takes a big chance, and nothing could be bigger, because God's entire reputation depends on the outcome. But love always requires taking a risk—love is exposed to rejection, neglect, abuse—even for God. Everything the name of God has ever meant in classical theology has depended upon God being the risk-free invulnerable rock of ages, the prime mover, the governor of the universe, the one with the vision to see everything and the power to steer it unto good. We have always counted on God. But how can God be there when needed if God is not there at all? How can God come to our rescue if no one's there to come? How can God be God if God rids God of God? What good is a rose when what we need is a rock or a sword?

The short answer is that in daring not to be, in daring to be nothing more than a kind of may-being, we are called upon to fill up what is lacking in the insistence of God. God allows the weight of existence to weigh in on us; the lightness of God's burden shifts the gravity of being to us. The burden of existence is on our shoulders, where everything that is done in and under the name of God takes place. God's insistent call requires our existing response. The name of God is the name of a powerless power by which a form of life is galvanized. The kingdom of God is what life would look like when the way we exist responds to what God insists. As I said at the beginning of this chapter, that is my point, the payoff of this entire exercise.

All this from love, for God is love and love, above all, is what is without why. If creation is a gift given from love, then religion cannot be a binding-back to God in which the gift is given back, the debt paid, and the divine action undone. God withdraws from existence in order to allow a smile to cross the surface of matter. The blossoming of the rose does not give glory *back* to God, which would annul the gift. Its blossoming *is* the glory of God. What greater love can someone have for their friends than to give up his or her being for them? The purity of God's insistence is that God is a promise, an unkept promise, and everything depends upon us to keep that promise, to translate that hope into reality. To say that God insists is to say that God is our hope, and that we hope to make this hope come true. To say that God is truth is to say that it falls upon us to make this truth come true.

Let me be clear that the inexistence of God is none of our doing; it belongs to God's own makeup for God to rid God of God, for God to free God from all this omnipotence and omniscience. It is God's own doing or un-doing, God's own atheism. It is not the result of some daring denial of God on our part, like the warrior atheists. These warriors need not have bothered. They are knocking on a door that is already open. God could have spared them the trouble and expense of raising an army. There is a divine and sublime atheism that precedes and supersedes their futile war on God and religion. Nor is God's inexistence the result of our indifference, of a failure to be mindful of the presence of God because of our selfish preoccupation with worldly concerns, like the bourgeois Christian culture castigated by Kierkegaard. It is not the result of our failure to know God or to comprehend God, of a learned unknowing or an unlearned one, or some unknowing that clouds God over, or a failure to acknowledge God.

God's inexistence is God's own affair, God's own (un-) doing. To add a dash of theological derring-do to an ancient formula, the essence of God lies in God's inexistence. That is what it means for God to be, or rather to not-be, or best of all, for God to insist, which is God's risky inexistence. We are asked to pick up where God leaves off. How? By making the kingdom of God come true, by the works of love, the works of mercy, by acts of unconditional hospitality and forgiveness. That is why I started out by talking about giving gifts unconditionally, without the expectation of a return. I was leading up to God.

Let me be still clearer that this is not the old Enlightenment, the old flat-footed atheism. The religion of the rose does not simply want to be rid of God pure and simple, but to let God rid God of God in such a way that something is still going on in the name of God. Something keeps coming back to haunt us, something that makes the world restless not *for* God but restless *with* God, coming from out of God's own restlessness, moved by God's inner and insistent disturbance. This is not a garden-variety atheism but a divine atheism, God's very own ridding God of God, one that belongs to the inner sanctum of theology itself, where the curtain parts and everyone is allowed to enter only to see—and this is the height of audacity—there is no being there, no entities at all, just a call, a voice in the dark.

In the religion of the rose, the proper theological appreciation of what is going on with God, the properly theological thing to say about God, is that God does not exist, God insists. Here many readers will hear the echoes of Paul Tillich, the father of a more radical or audacious theology, who said that, to the assertion that God is an existent entity, "atheism is the right religious and theological reply."[8] But for Tillich and for me that is not the end of theology but the beginning. Tillich goes on to say that God is not a being because God is the ground of beings. By this he means an infinite womb or matrix from which finite beings emerge and into which they return, while God, as the ground of the comings and goings of these beings, abides forever. I think that Tillich is to that extent still in a residual alliance with the old palace God, except that this time God has come down to earth and mixed with the commoners.

In the religion modeled after the rose, God must rid God-self even of the ground of being and consent to being a ground-less ground, as exposed as the rest of us to the restlessness in things. So to Tillich's assertion that God is the underlying ground of beings, the proper theological response is also athe-ism, but not the atheism of warrior atheists. Instead it is God's own atheism. The audacity of God is that God is an atheist, too, even about the ground of being. God is neither the High-est Being, nor being's ground, but the unconditional call that solicits being, a disturbance rumbling within being, not a rock but a crack or crevice; not a juncture but a disjoining, a rup-ture; not a plenum but a gap; not the gap God fills but the gap God opens. The name of God is the name of a deep restless-ness that inserts itself in being, that makes being restless with becoming and with longing for the future. God inserts Godself insistently, insidiously inside being and exposes being to its outside, calling for the future, for the coming of the future, while also recalling an immemorial past. The only "might" of God of which we might speak is the might of might-be. God's only being is may-being, which is what it means to say that God does not exist, that God calls, that God does not exist, God insists.

Giving God a Chance

My idea is not to attack religion but to offer an alternate version of religion, to repeat religion differently. That bit of impudence goes back to the mid-1980s, when it hit the professor in me that the thematics of the "other" in Continental philosophy was a line taken straight from Jesus, whose preaching turned on the way the kingdom of God settles upon the outcast and the outsider. Whether they knew it or not, these bearded elbow-patched philosophers, otherwise oozing with their odium for theology, might as well have been Appalachian Bible-thumpers! They were stealing lines from Jesus left and right![9] I came to speak of a poetics of the kingdom of God and have referred to it as a "sacred anarchy," meaning that the rule of God is found in the rule of the unruly, of what Paul called the nothings and nobodies (1 Cor. 1:28). That divine unruliness is integral to what I now find myself saying about the insistence of God and the nihilism of grace.

The Little Church has never missed a chance to make the point that we need God. But in this alternate way of thinking about God, in a Big Church or Religionless Church, it is no less true that God needs us, that without us God cannot be God. Without us nothing is going on in the name of God. God dares to abstain from existing, to remain coiled up in a call that precedes being, that solicits being. God takes the chance of calling upon us uninvited, depending upon us precisely when everything is at stake, leaving the kingdom of God at the mercy of our response. God's Kingdom is run by the unruliness of grace, where the divinity of God depends upon the sheer fortuitousness that this call will be heard, the summons heeded, that someone will read and heed a message in a bottle of unknown provenance. God is being left to the mercy of chance, of the chance of a response. God's chance in the world depends on us.

God's love is to relinquish God's most powerful weapon, the bargaining chip that gave God all his leverage in the past, the omnipotence that reduced creation to the fear of retaliation by an angry and almighty deity and the desire for eternal rewards by an appeased deity. God rolls the dice on us. God's love is doing all this *gratis*, for nothing. God abdicates all such exaltation and depends solely upon an audacious grace, on the chance that something will get itself done in and under what solicits us in and under the name (of) "God," which floats over us on the wings of a dove. The name of God is the name of a chance for grace. The sole chance for God is that something will be mobilized, set in motion, moved without a prime mover, caused without a first cause, which to all the world looks mad. To all the world the people of God look like people dancing to music no one else can hear. God dares to take a chance. The chance God takes, God's wager, is to leave all this to the chance of a response to an appeal that can be simply rejected without appeal. When I speak of the weakness of God I mean the weak force of a call. I do not mean an entity whose being is otherwise intact but whose power is weak, as if God had good intentions but no will to carry them out, or as if God is a divine being missing one of the divine names we have hitherto attributed to him, like a person who has lost a limb. I mean the powerless power, the unforced force, of a call.

A call can be cultivated as a call only if it is kept in an optimally weak mode, not allowed to swell into the authoritative command of an omnipotent being. It belongs to the very structure of a genuine call to call with a certain subtlety, a barely audible audacity, by leaving us all in the dark about who or what is calling and who or what is being called for, about who or what is being recalled.[10] It is not a case of an identifiable caller with unimpeachable credentials passing along an urgent order or a piece of vital information. This call is not far from anxiety, but the anxiety is not pathological but salutary, the awakening of freedom standing before the abyss of the possible.

This is not just the ghost of old Feuerbach again. I have not spent a lifetime in consultation with Jackie, Brother Paul, the other Jackie, and numerous other correspondents, all of us together thinking this through, staying up late into the night—in order to end up repeating Feuerbach! I am not saying that God is a "projection" of human perfections on an infinite screen in the sky—as if we empty our real human selves into a fiction called "God." God, what is going on in the name of God, is not a projection but a projectile headed straight at us, a missile upending our narcissistic desires, a visitation that comes without invitation. The name of God is the way we nominate something that calls and prevails upon us with unrelenting insistence, something that is not our idea, that keeps at us and gives us no rest. It comes, but we didn't invite it. The calls comes as an inbreaking claim, a plea, a prayer, for the gift or hospitality, not as our prayer to God but as God's prayer to us, God's taking a chance on us. God needs us to make the being of God come true, God weeping over Jerusalem, every Jerusalem, wherever it is found anywhere in the world. God belongs to a different order than being or existence or power, not because God is nothing but a projection of ours, but because God calls from before being to beyond being. God belongs not to the indicative order but to the order of the subjunctive, of what might or ought or should be. God belongs not to the nominal order but to the invocative or provocative order; not to the ontological order but to the hauntological. God is bold enough to settle for being a spirit, a spirit bold enough to dare be content with being a specter, a shadowy thing that neither is nor is not, that dares to be no more than a might-be. But this provocation is no more a projection of ours than is a work of literature, a work of "fiction," which visits upon us the painful truth of our mortality and leaves us trembling in the night.

God rids God of God in the name of God, in order to take a chance that the existence of God will unfold in the world, that the kingdom of God will come true. The name of God is the name of a promise to the world that we are called upon to keep. It is the name of a memory of a world that we are called upon to recall, the memory of an immemorial call, meaning that we are called upon to answer a call we have never heard. The name of God is the name of a promise and a memory of the world, of a world yearning to be born. The inexistence of God does not spell the death of God but sings of a God groaning to be born. Letting the world be the world means that what is called for in the name of God will come true, that we will make it come true, which is the chance God takes on us.

I admit to serving up an unauthorized reading of the Scriptures, which I treat as if they were texts found in a cave whose authors are unknown, which we read because of what they have to say, not because we are told they dropped from the sky. I am not even going to apply to the Chancellery Office for an *Imprimatur*. To rid God of God is to let God dissolve without remainder into narratives about God, which it is up to us to actualize, to leave it to us to make these stories of unknown provenance come true. God's Word dares to disappear into words, into parables given for us to ponder, to be no more than suggestions for us to entertain, puzzles to puzzle out. God's word fades into free-floating possibilities for us actualize, templates for an audacious life. God recedes into strange stories about what the world would look like if God were to rule instead of the politicians who serve the interests of the money that got them elected so that they may be reelected. God's insistence is to be content to be an anonymous author, even a pseudonymous or fictional author, of amazing stories of old, back in the day when prophets and miracle men strode the earth. God's insistence is to be an unknown poet, a spinner of tall tales and unbelievable yarns, where whales swallow fellows whole who later on emerge unscathed, and where little mustard seeds scattered here and there grow into mighty trees and kingdoms. God's insistence is to populate these sacred stories with purely fictional characters, without cost to their veracity, daring to let them be true with another and deeper truth, with a truth of another order, and thus to be a contribution to a poetics of insistence where the truth is up to us. When it comes to the deep truth of narratives, the distinction between fact and fictions collapses in upon itself and it makes no difference who the author is.

In the world, the almighty sword of God's might is hammered into the plowshare of might-be; God's being is modified into may-being, God's wealth into poverty, God's necessity into "perhaps," God's Providence into a chance for God. By transferring God's infinite wealth into the accounts of the world, God's infinite actuality is redistributed into the endless possibilities that proliferate across space and time. God's audacity is to turn away the blazing glory of the divine countenance in order to let the light of a little smile appear on the surface of matter in a remote corner of the universe. God's light is like the warm glow of a cabin hearth on a snowy night in a remote corner of the woods, like a rose blossoming in a field of snow.

Without God we can do nothing, but then again without us God can do nothing. Without us, nothing gets done in the name of God, since the name of God is the name of a call for something to be done by us. So we each need each other, God and the world, which is why Kierkegaard's Johannes Climacus said that the name of God is the name of a deed. God's need for us is God's need for deeds to actualize the divine call. The weakness of God is to be translated into the strength of our resolve to fill up what is missing in the body of God. Otherwise the name of God is sounding brass and a tinkling cymbal. It comes down to deeds, or rather it spirals up to and breaks out into deeds, like Martha making ready for the coming of Jesus. In the kingdom of God, there are things to be made and things to be done, where the people of God are as defenseless as a sheep among wolves, as wise as a serpent, as innocent as a dove (Matt. 10:16).

To rid God of God means that God, setting aside the pomp of being and all its glories as nothing to boast about (Phil. 2:6), has so loved the world (John 3:16) as to give the world the chance to become the world it promises to be, to fill up what is lacking in the body of God (Col. 1:24).

■ ■ ■

That, God help me, is where I have ended up. If I am wrong here, there will be hell to pay in the hereafter, "if there is one," which is the way the other Jackie always liked to put it, whenever his demon warned him he was being too dogmatic.

Thus do I adjudicate among the various voices that have been conducting an internal dialogue within myself, this boisterous committee where everybody has an opinion, no one is willing to yield the floor, and it is almost impossible to form a majority, this polyphony within me that I call with no little pretense my "self." If you stand outside the room and listen you will hear the voices of Jackie and Brother Paul and the Professor, of Aquinas and Heidegger, of Augustine and Hegel, and of course the other Jackie, in a polyvocal game of Jacks that leaves me confused. When I play back the recording, I cannot tell who is doing the talking, who is saying what to whom. The one thing I am sure of is that this is not going to play well in the little churches. The one thing I am praying for is that a lot of other people in other bigger churches—there is no such thing as "the" Church—recognize this story very well. They know all about the weakness of God, the insistence of God, the being inside/outside religion, a religionless religion, a proto-religion, a religion with/out religion. Together, without knowing one another, we form a community without community, otherwise known as the Spirit/spirit/specter of God.

Interlude: A Short Nocturnal Seminar

Jackie: I think it has finally happened.

Brother Paul: What has happened?

Jackie: I think you have not only lost our vocation for us, you have lost our soul.

Brother Paul: I did no such thing. I did not lose our vocation. I was faithful to it. I saw it through to the end. It was the right thing at the right time, but end it did, and then I moved us on to the next stage so that we could continue our vocation but by another means. A vocation, after all, is a calling that we spend a lifetime trying to discern. But all along, from the very earliest memories any of us have had, it has always been about what is calling and what is called for in and under the name of God.

Jackie: But you do not believe that God exists.

Brother Paul: I don't think you are talking to me now. I think you mean the Professor. You cannot pin any of this on me. When I took my leave of the Brothers, I did not see this coming, what the Professor was going to say, not at all.

Professor: Truth to tell, neither did I. But I understand what you are saying, Jackie, I really do. Don't forget. I have been there. You and I are not really different, you know.

Jackie: How can you say a thing like that?

Professor: The stars, Jackie, the stars. You know what I mean, and so does Brother Paul. None of us can deny those starry thoughts. We are all in this together, always have been.

Jackie: But you know very well that I was not thinking anything as crazy as all this stuff. It was just a passing thought and I never thought anything like what you are saying. I thought the stars were all just part of God's mystery.

Professor: You certainly never said what I said. I'll give you that. How could you? You never met the other Jackie, but you would have liked him if you had. He's the one that loosened my tongue.

Jackie: He should have taught you to bite your lip!

Professor: I think we all know, all three of us, what is going on, and has been going on, from very early on.

Brother Paul: He's right about this much, Jackie. If you spend as many hours of lonely prayer as I did you get to thinking a lot of strange thoughts. You know I actually got calluses on my knees from all that time in chapel? Did I ever tell you two that? Anyway, once in a while, I wasn't going to announce it to the Director of Novices, but sometimes I would wonder, What is really going on? We would rise really early, when the stars were still out, and I would wonder, does anybody know we're here? So I think he's right to say that the only difference between you and me and the Professor is that he has spelled it out in a way we didn't dare or even know how to go about.

Professor: It has always been about the stars, Jackie, and about God, about daring to think God, and about a more radical faith that the Little Church contains but, then again, cannot contain. I mean really daring to think what's going on with God. All I have ever tried to do is get to the bottom of what God has been doing to us, and doing for us, the three of us.

Brother Paul: Like when Meister Eckhart says we should let God be God in us?

Professor: Exactly. To let God be God means first to see that God does not get puffed up into a Big Being somewhere, up above or down below, and then to see that does not mean there is nothing to God. That's more of a picture or a story about God, the one we started with. Don't get me wrong. Stories are important, and that is a gripping story—we can all testify to that—but like any story it needs to be interpreted. My bet is all three of us see this—that what is going on in the name of God is the pull of a promise, the lure or dream of something unimaginable, a hope against hope. The name of God is the name of a way to be, a way of living in the world, where things are a lot riskier than we all thought. Life's a beautiful risk.

Jackie: And a frightening one.

Professor: You tell me that every night and, trust me, I hear you. I am telling you the truth when I say that you and I are not really different. You are with me, Jackie, night and day, even, especially when I don my professional cap and make it sound like I know what I am talking about. Don't think I don't see you smiling at me.

Jackie: So where does that leave us? You're the one who has read all those books, and who keeps quoting these strange French philosophers you like so much. What now? We trusted you. Explain to me how you haven't just ruined everything for us.

Brother Paul: To tell you the truth, I share that concern. What are we to do now? What's going to become of us? After all, you're the one who got us into this jam.

Professor: You're not making it easy for me. You never have. I remember everything the two of you said over the years, almost everything anyway, my memory is not as good as yours. I want you to know that you mean the world to me and that I love you both. You know that, right? I mean I am trying to be faithful to you both, to speak from the heart, from our heart, trying to speak for all of us. So let's go back one more time to the story of the stars. I think we can all agree, that's our story. I say our story, but I have a hunch that it's really everybody's story. Anyway, much as I love these talks we have every night, you're right. I have to answer your questions and I am going to have to break this session off now and don my professorial cap and gown again.

Then the Lord God said,
"See, the man has become like one of us, knowing good and evil;
and now, he might reach out his hand
and take also from the tree of life, and eat, and live forever"
—therefore the Lord God sent him forth from the garden of Eden,
to till the ground from which he was taken.
He drove out the man;
and at the east of the garden of Eden
he placed the cherubim, and a sword flaming and turning
to guard the way to the tree of life.
—(Gen. 3:22-24)

What a piece of work is a man!
How noble in reason, how infinite in faculty!
In form and moving how express and admirable!
In action how like an angel,
in apprehension how like a god!
—*Hamlet*, II, 2

CHAPTER SEVEN

Guarding the Way to the Tree of Life: From Angelology to Technology

What we have been discussing up to now is what the philosophers call the problem of nihilism. Now the time has come in these final chapters to face the music, to spell out a bit more exactly, how I mean to address the question of cosmic meaninglessness by means of what I am calling the nihilism of grace, which I call, at least on odd-numbered days, my religion.

I described this religionless religion as a hymn to the earth. I am prepared to admit that, cosmically considered, this hymn is no more than the faint sounding of a song off in a distant corner of the universe, like a siren slowly receding out of earshot as it races away from us, terminating in silence. By silence I mean absolute silence, not human silence, which we can hear, which can be "pregnant" or "telling," but the sheer silence of the inhuman, where there is nothing left to hear and no one left to hear it. I have all along been building up to this, trying to see our lives from the perspective of the inhuman future described by Lyotard, of the cold black night of solar destruction. Even that chilling description is an anthropomorphism. In the inhuman, there will be no flesh left to shiver, or sight left to be blinded by the dark, no day or night at all, no black or white. This thought is unthinkable to Plato for whom the sun was both the substance and the symbol of the everlasting. But it is no less a rebuke to the Platonism in us all, anyone for whom the sun's warmth and light and seeming imperishability is the reassuring image of the eternal, of everything good and true and beautiful, of God on high.

Faced with the thought of the faceless death of thought, with the utterly posthuman, nonhuman, inhuman end that lies in store for us, what hope is there for hope? In what can we hope? Having been deprived of the resources of omnipotence to deal with an approaching nihilism, having arrived at the battlefield armed only with a rose, the time has come to face the question: *If God rids God of God, what is to become of us?*

The Technological Option and the Tree of Life

Of the two ways to address the prospect of the inhuman discussed by Lyotard, the first is the advice given by Epicurus. That is basically to drop the subject. Behave like the politicians, table the motion for consideration later, knowing full well that later never comes, at least not during our term of office. The posthuman condition will postdate us and is of no consequence here and now, where there are more pressing matters to deal with. The second is to seek the technological resources to escape the fate of this doomed planet and head for higher (or outer) cosmic ground. The first proposal makes abstract rational sense, but that is precisely what is so wrong with it. Pure reason has no sense and even less sensibility. It is much too much like what titillated the Enlightenment philosophers but leaves the rest of us stone cold. It has a kind of formal bare-bones rationality, a skeletal logic that might appeal to a half human/half Vulcan like Mr. Spock in *Star Trek* but is of little use to full-blooded human beings who can no more ignore the future than they can ignore the law of gravity.

We are beings of hope and aspiration, turned by something inside of us toward the future, and there is no turning aside from that. To be human is to hope, and to hope is to affirm the future, and the future is the coming of what we cannot see coming. Trying not to think of the future is like trying not to think of the white elephant sitting across from us in the dentist's waiting room working on his laptop.

That is why Lyotard's other proposal, the technological proposal, makes more sense, and that is the one we want to consider in this chapter. Faced with death, everything in us resists. Faced with death, *in extremis*, we take extreme measures. Nothing is too audacious if the alternative is extinction. Our preference for the second alternative over Epicurus's has been borne out by the facts on the ground, by the actual course of history, where we have enthusiastically embraced the technological option in no uncertain terms. From the dawning days of modernity, we have sought to cheat death by waging a techno-scientific war on it aimed at pushing it back, postponing it, extending life. We do everything we can to buy ourselves more time, maybe even to come up with something that will vanquish death altogether! Today, contemporary genetics has given that project wings. We are hard at work on a kind of techno-immortality project, a "Methuselah Project,"[1] which would dramatically extend biological life expectancy, maybe even into several centuries. But even more radically, we are attempting to escape biology altogether, to relieve life of its dependence upon its fragile biological base and, in principle, of its dependence upon the balmy climes of planet Earth.

It is not an accident that Methuselah is a biblical figure. It is a crucial tip-off. Techno-science is stepping in where only theology dared to tread. Genetics is picking up where Genesis leaves off. Technology today moves in an eerie proximity to theology, both of which have set out with the same objective, to cheat death so that we can be numbered among the immortals. But isn't this exactly what Yahweh feared, which led him "to guard the way to the tree of life?" Immortality was not part of the plan. Death, *pace* St. Augustine, was not a punishment for "original sin" in the second creation story. On the contrary, it was precisely the desire to escape death and achieve immortality, to eat of the second tree, the tree of life, that earned Adam and Eve their walking papers. That implies that the original plan was that they would *not* live forever, *not* have eternal life. It was for fear that they would conceive such a desire that Yahweh drove the two of them out of the garden and placed an angel, armed with a blazing sword, to guard the tree of life (Gen. 3:22-24), lest these two ever have the audacity to make a run at it.

Yahweh's wishes to the contrary notwithstanding, the Little Church was not about to give up on immortality. Immortality does all the heavy lifting in the economy of the Little Church. But the curious thing today is that now the theologians have competition. While theologians today are busy stressing their attentiveness to this world, the physicists of today are in search of another world of ghostly quantum phenomena that eye hath not seen nor ear heard. There the everyday notion of matter is considered quaint but rather crass; 85 percent of the matter in the universe is invisible (dark), while AI scientists have dreams of immortality dancing in their head. But of course this techno-theological immortality will only serve to make the pious panic.

To be sure, the theologians do want to become gods—but they want God to make us gods, not science! I think that Yahweh saw both of them coming, the theologians and the physicists, and warned them both against it. I told you so, Yahweh roars. They want to live forever and be like us. I warned them against that, but they are doing it anyway. Well, they will have to get past my cherubim first. The sheer audacity! I regret the day I made them! (Gen. 6:6).

In one of the most famous of the Psalms (8:4-6), which praises the majesty of God's creation, the majestic sweep of the moon and the stars, the psalmist asks in rhetorical wonder, what are human beings that God should be mindful of them? Then he praises God for making us just a little less than the angels and giving us dominion over the earth. Actually, the author of the Letter to the Hebrews, citing this passage (2:7), spoke of "angels" (*angelous*), following the Greek Septuagint translation. The original Hebrew, however, said "gods," "divinities," "divine beings" (*Elohim*), in the plural, presumably making reference to the idea in Genesis that we were made in the image of God, but it also recalls the prohibition on eating of the tree of life.

Let us stay with "angels," the Greek New Testament version, because that's the one with a history. God made us a little less than the angels but, just as Yahweh feared, we have had the audacity to try to make up the difference between our mortality and their immortality. It is as if we have always suffered from a terrible case of angel-envy and now more than ever before we seek to close the distance between the angels and us, between immortality and us. Angels are classic elements of religion. They constantly show up in our art and our stories; to this very day they are alive and well in Alabama and among the Christian Right generally. But today it is science that, dare I say, is hell bent on making us their equal and slipping past Yahweh's guard.

The Enlightenment "dare to think" (*sapere aude*) has led to the audacity of technology, of the info-techno-angelology of the "information age," which is making a run on the tree of life. The irony is palpable: Lyotard's technological option turns out to be surprisingly close to the option he never so much as mentions, presumably on the grounds that it merits only our unreserved incredulity—religion, theology, and the afterlife! Methuselah turns out to be the patron saint of technology, of nothing less than a new—and improved?—immortality project. Theology and technology should merge faculties—as they are both working on the same project, to live forever. They are both trying to become like the angels, to cheat death and boast with Paul, "O death, where is thy victory?" (1 Cor. 15:55). That is the primal boast of theology, even if eating of the tree of life was precisely *not* Yahweh's idea.

Hope is the affirmation of the future, and our future is going to be transformed by technology in ways we cannot even imagine. Is technology the new theology? Is technology proving to be the way the prayers of theology will be answered? Is technology what theology has all along been talking about—but in a purely imaginative mode and without the mathematics to understand itself? Is technology where our hope lies? If not, is all hope lost? Are we then out of options?

Angels, Smart Phones, and the Future

The analogy between contemporary technology and classical angelology is not a mere curiosity, like noticing a cloud that looks like a horse. It is a touchstone phenomenon of the technological project that has been explored brilliantly by Michel Serres, a French philosopher who taught at Stanford University for many years.[2] Like a lot of good ideas, it sounds far-fetched until we think about it. To begin with, the Greek word *angelos* simply means "messenger," and the angels were basically instant-message systems devised by the authors of the scriptures. The first book Serres wrote was about Hermes, the Greek god of communication and the namesake of contemporary hermeneutics. With the advent of Christianity, Hermes lost his job to the angels, who today appear to be losing their job to smart phones and hand-held devices. In the Bible, when God needed to communicate with humans, and particularly when the divinity was in a supernatural hurry, the angels were his agents of choice. When God decided that Abraham was willing to go through with the sacrifice of Isaac, God had to get an instant message to the Patriarch to put down his dagger and not harm the boy—so he dispatched an angel to the scene. Nowadays the Almighty could have texted him. A contemporary painting of this famous biblical story would portray an anxious Isaac watching as his father reads a text message he has just received on his smart phone.

Furthermore, as we can learn from any Renaissance painting, where angels are depicted with the wings of birds—a "divinanimal" image, the other Jackie would say[3]—angels are well known for their powers of *flight*. Angelic messages are delivered by airmail. So Serres pairs a number of famous paintings of angels with wings outspread with the strikingly similar poses of modern jet aircraft on the opposing page. (It's a philosophical cocktail table book that will impress any visitors to your home with your sophistication!) Angels could fly at the "speed of thought," the medieval theologians said. We today would speak instead of the speed of light, but the idea is the same: instant travel, or as close as can be gotten to it.

Again, among the most sacred assignments of the angels was their work as *guardians* of human beings, helping mortals wend their way through the maze and craze of space and time, a function taken over today by global positioning systems, which are becoming more and more powerful and more intimately woven into our lives. These electronic guardian angels are already being implanted in automobile windshields and eyeglasses (and maybe eventually in our brains).

Angels are also famous for their blazing *intelligence*, where everything is understood in a flash, no need to piece it together from sensible data, as do humans. The supercomputers of today store astonishing amounts of information delivered with an equally blazing speed, calculating in seconds what it would take unaided human intelligence centuries to accomplish, and there is always a new generation of computers on the horizon as the computer engineers rack their brains to find something faster and more powerful. As Homer Simpson once complained, isn't there anything faster than a microwave? Again, we are beginning to imagine how to implant that information directly in our brains. Were we to come up with a way do this with foreign languages—about the only way we will get Americans to learn one!—or with instant translation systems, we would effectively reproduce the miracle of Pentecost, the gift of tongues, given to the disciples so that they could spread the good news to all nations. When God issues his fiat in Genesis, or when Jesus cures the paralytics with a word, we have here early prototype models of "voice activation." Next comes mind activation, which will eventually allow the handicapped to move paralyzed or artificial limbs, repeating other biblical miracles. There's more: the early moderns liked to mock medieval angelologists by asking, "How many angels can dance on the head of a pin?" Let us slightly alter that question and ask, How much information can you store on increasingly miniaturized microchips? Mock that!

Information technology is the "repetition" of angelology. The same underlying concerns that were in play when our world was populated with angels and demons are now being replayed in a new and surprising way in a world populated with ghostly gluons and bosons. Technology recapitulates angelology. What is being figured in angelic life is being figured out in a way no one saw coming—in technology.

The most striking thing of all, in my view, is that this info-technological angelic project is an *immortality* project. For "information" is not only a technology today; it is an ontology. It is not just how we *do* things; it is, we are beginning to think, what we *are*, what everything *is*—from subatomic particles to Fundamentalists! Consider the point that, beyond what they *do*, angels *are* ontologically spiritual beings, which was the occasion of an interesting debate in the Middle Ages. Thomas Aquinas argued that the angels were purely spiritual substances (all form, no matter) while the Franciscans argued that, as created beings, angels must have some kind of bodily makeup, albeit of a very light and airy sort, unlike the gross heavy bodies humans have. Angels sound a little bit like neutrinos—very ghostly, almost immaterial, infinitesimally small particles—which it was recently claimed, falsely it turns out, might actually travel faster than the speed of light. Talk about a "God particle"! The Franciscan theologians, who did not know much about neutrinos, said angelic bodies are swift because they are all air and fire, no earth and water, so the Franciscans had the basic idea: mostly energy, not much mass. That, according to a very good New Testament scholar, is probably what Paul meant in 1 Corinthians 15 when he referred to the resurrected body as a *soma pneumatikon*, a spiritual body; on the last day we shed our corruptible, gross, wet-heavy bodies for incorruptible, finer, lighter dry-hot ones, in which we can flit about freely for all eternity.[4]

Exactly how far is that from the dreams of contemporary robotologists to "upload" consciousness from our present corruptible biologically based bodies and download them into shiny new incorruptible robot bodies?[5] Of course, we will still have to keep an eye out for magnets and we must be sure to make a backup copy in case of an accident, rather like the Cylons in *Battlestar Gallactica*, who try never to get too far from a "resurrection ship" in case of an unexpected death, where the rules of Cylon triage dictate the dead are first in line for emergency treatment! We see something similar in the 2014 film *Transcendence*, where the intelligence of Dr. Will Caster (Johnny Depp), the foremost expert in the world on AI, is "uploaded" into the Internet, allowing him to transcend his mortal body.

That would meet the conditions set by Lyotard for slipping out of the solar system before the sun dies. The body, Lyotard says, is the hardware; language and thought are the software, and that distinction is displacing the old imaginative distinction between the material and the immaterial! So we need new hardware to make this escape possible, which is exactly what the robotologists are working on. John Polkinghorne, the Anglican priest and quantum physicist, speculates that Christian "resurrection" might be thought of as a process in which God first uploads our software onto the divine hardware until such time (Judgment Day) as God can supply us with new hardware, with shiny new incorruptible maintenance-free bodies.[6] In Polkinghorne's bit of "info-techno-theology," the analogy of angelology and technology was never closer: two versions of the posthuman, a technological one and a theological one.

Border Breakdowns and the Advent of the Inhuman

These are portraits of a very unnerving inhuman future. If hope is always hope in a precarious future, we are at present in a particularly precarious position. Our unprotected exposure to the promise and the threat of the future was never more acute than today. Our hope is always that the future is worth more, but experience proves that in fact it often turns out to be worse, sometimes even a monster, which is certainly what the word "inhuman" suggests. At the onset of the "age of information," things appear poised to undergo a staggering transformation, affecting every aspect of our lives, opening up an amazing but frightening future. A sea change is underway reaching all the way down to very definition of birth and death, maternity and paternity, the technological and the biological, and pushing up against the very limits of our mortality.

We are engaged in risky business. Kant said that "Enlightenment" represents human beings coming of age, but as usual with Enlightenment thinkers, that may have been a bit optimistic. We risk behaving more like teenagers with sky-high testosterone readings. We have the feeling that we are on threshold of what people call the "posthuman," at the onset of something extraordinarily different. A hundred years from now, or five hundred, all these marvels will look horse-and-carriage quaint, ridiculously old-fashioned. Our descendants will smile with condescension at life back in the day when we were still "earthlings," when the advanced information systems of today will look like life in a medieval village.

What is going on today has been nicely described by Donna Haraway as a series of three "border breakdowns." First, the border between the human and the technological. Haraway scared the daylights out of the humanists many years ago with an audacious article, later a book, claiming that we were becoming "cyborgs."[7] A cyborg is a border-breaker—and a gender-bender—if ever there were one, a heterogeneous mix of the natural and the artificial, of natural life and artificial life, of natural intelligence and artificial intelligence, as our bodies and minds are more and more supplemented by "artificial" limbs and organs, implants and supplements, raising the question of whether and what the limits between the technological and the biological are.

Secondly, the border between humans and "animals" is disappearing fast as we gradually surrender our exclusive anthropocentric privileges and realize both that animals also have rights and that humans are animals, which is one of the things I like about Martha's attention to the bodily needs of Jesus. We begin to appreciate how very human the animals are (do they smile?) and how very much an animal the human is. Whatever our specific difference is, it is not to be thought of as pure "rationality" dropping down from above upon a generic "animal" substrate lying down below. The human does not take leave of or supersede the animal; it inflects the animal in a specifically human way.

Finally, we are witness to a breakdown of the ancient distinction between matter and spirit. That distinction has had a long run. It got kicked off when Plato distinguished the sensible world of space and time (to which our bodies belong) from the supersensible world of the eternal forms (where our souls belong). It got theological teeth when that distinction was wedded with the biblical distinction between heaven and earth. The result was "Christian Neoplatonism," whose high point was St. Augustine's famous distinction between the city of man and the city of God. That distinction, which has had remarkable survival value, is a pre-Copernican, prescientific, and impressionistic construction, a work of "strong imagination,"[8] to cite the Bard. It has exercised hegemonic influence in religion ever since, up to the point of being treated as more or less identical with religion. But it is my perversity to argue that it is a picture, a trope, a figure, that bears up less and less well under close analysis, earning greater and greater "incredulity" with each passing day.

It used to be that the best way to taunt the pious was to declare that we are machines. But that point was difficult to sustain when what you had in mind was the clunky, noisy, smelly, mechanical machines of the old industrial revolution, with its chains and pulleys and smokestacks. It becomes a lot more unnerving if what you mean is a complex and subtle informational system packaged in beautifully designed electronic devices, and if instead of body and spirit you simply distinguish hardware and software. As Lyotard says, technology was not invented by humans; humans were invented by evolutionary technology. Any material system, including and especially a living one, is technological: "it filters information useful to its survival."

The difference that makes a difference with humans is that when it comes to information, we are omnivorous. Our memory capacity is enormous and we have a meta-systematic ability to move back and forth among many different systems and codes, which gives us a relative independence from our environment. The distinction between the material and the immaterial is collapsing. Informational systems represent a third and somewhat ghostly thing, neither the one nor the other. No one saw them coming in the nineteenth century, back in the day when the old wars between freedom and determinism, lithesome spirit and clunky matter, pure idealism and brute materialism filled the air.

The unnerving thing is this. As Lyotard points out, completely up-to-date and technologically literate philosophers maintain that, just as are we not machines with gears and pulleys, so too we are not digital computers either.[9] We do not compute with digits, long strings of 1s and 0s, inside narrow parameters governed by algorithms. Indeed these very programs must be written by the intelligent imaginative human beings who devise and program the computers and who do not themselves think in terms of long strings of 1s and 0s.

The new AI scientists agree: our brains do not work like that. But instead of taking that as a stake in the heart of the project of artificial intelligence, computer technologists today have taken it to heart. They regard it as an insight that should guide the work of computer technology. Several remarkable transformations are now taking place in the very nature of computer processing. "Quantum computers" follow quantum rules, like superposition, not classical rules, upon which the "bits" of "classical" computers are based; quantum computers allow for bits that could be 1 or 0 or both at the same time.[10] At the same time, an exciting but unnerving shift from statistical to biological computation is underway, abandoning the fundamental model that has been in place ever since the basic ideas of modern computers were worked out back in 1950s. A contemporary computer scientist says that this shift "reflects the *Zeitgeist*. Everyone knows there is something big happening, and they're trying to find out what it is." (Hegel could not have put it better.) The occasion of these remarks was a report that the most popular class on campus at Stanford University was a graduate course on biological computational systems that had attracted some 760 students—while the humanities programs report that they are home to fewer and fewer students.[11]

Accordingly the AI scientists are seeking to fundamentally redesign the way that computers function, ever more closely reproducing the way that our brains work, imitating the way that neurons build neural networks, which means that the computers will learn to correct their own mistakes. Instead of the current mode of processing, computer scientists are developing "neuromorphic processors," which make use of neuron-like elements that imitate brain synapses.[12] Instead of mechanical programming, the processors are "weighted," which allows them to shift with changing data. That is what we humans call "learning from experience." Might we be able to program the computers to *hope*, to *resist* the weight of past experience? Biological "computing" becomes the model for artificial computing, and the more we learn about the brain, the better the artificial intelligence will be. These processors will also eliminate computer crashes, which are caused when only one element in the entire system corrupts. Neuromorphic processors can tolerate errors by adapting to the unexpected; the algorithms are simply altered with the alteration.

The computers are starting to take account of the event! The computer scientists are paying attention to deconstruction! What is emerging is neither purely mechanical nor immaterial, but a subtle airy-light flow of information. The Franciscan angelology was right: underlying the gross objects of ordinary experience are the airy-light operations of the subatomic particles. They are not two different worlds, but, as Hegel said, the same world in two different states, which, back in the day, were imaginatively pictured as "spirit" and "matter," the "city of God" and the "world."

Monsters

The question of hope turns on still another aspect of this analogy: angels come both good and bad. Angels, who are agents of peace and love, are also famous, or infamous, for going over to the dark side, and when they do, they *really* do, and then we call them demons. Our hope is always that the future is worth more, but experience proves it often turns out to be worse. So is technology going to be the Sabbath of life—or is it going to be our worst nightmare? Is all this going to be "good news," which is of course more angel-speak ("evangelical" = *eu*, "good," + *angelos*). Or are there bad angels in the making, maybe even a monster? The answer of course is it may be either one, or maybe some measure of both. There may be dragons. Nobody is guaranteeing anything. Maybe the real monsters are coming under the name of the "posthuman," compounded of the human and the inhuman. "Be careful what you pray for" when we find ourselves hesitating before the next experiment.

We stand before a future that is creepy, uncanny, spooky, positively eerie, which means our *Geist* may be ghastly, as in *Poltergeist*! We hope for an utterly utopian future, putting dazzling technological marvels at our daily disposal, a Sabbath of rest in which the machines do all the work, but we know better. So we also worry that it will be monstrous and dystopian, realizing all of the worst fears we have harbored ever since they were first formulated two centuries ago by Mary Shelley in her prophetic *Frankenstein* (1818), perhaps the most famous monster in modern Western literature. Maybe Yahweh was right to guard the way to the tree of life. Maybe we should keep our hands off immortality.

The new technologies will relieve us of the drudgery of routinized work—while reducing the workforce and accentuating the divide between people who have access to them and people who do not. They will make it difficult for totalitarian states to control the flow of images of police brutality or the military suppression of popular protests—even as Big Brother now takes a new digital form as Big Data. Our fascination with robots that "learn" from their mistakes is mixed with the horror that they might get to the point where we won't realize they *are* robots. Or that *they* won't! That they might communicate with each other in a language *we* cannot understand. Science fiction does not look quite so fictitious any longer—remember the way that HAL asserted his independence in *2001: A Space Odyssey*, the musical score of which was taken from Richard Strauss's "Thus Spoke Zarathustra." But might it not turn out that instead of the "superhuman" (*Übermensch*) predicted by Nietzsche we will end up with the inhuman?

Might we hit the point that the computers will start creating the computers and organically based life will be relegated to permanent second-class status? Is our organic life not basically just a very complex information system run by our DNA that is not in principle different from the artificial intelligence systems that today are trying to mime them and tomorrow might replace them? Might it be that we ourselves, and our organic life, are short-timers, that we will at some distant point replace our biological bodies with robot bodies?

We do not know just how much success this attempt on the part of technology to realize angelology will meet. Perhaps our distant descendants really will find some way to escape Spaceship Earth and relocate elsewhere before we are overtaken by the solar disaster. The first eerie signs of it have already appeared, when NASA confirmed in 2013 that the Voyager 1 spacecraft had left the solar system the year before and hence that something made with human hands was actually traveling in interstellar space! Here instead of Europeans crossing the Atlantic to discover a "new world," a human artifact crossed beyond the gravitational pull of the sun in interstellar travel. Something made by us no longer found "under the sun," which is Ecclesiastes' favorite trope. Were the human race itself able to accomplish such a thing, life "back on Earth" would become part of posthuman lore. Stories would be passed down by our posthuman descendants about life back in the day when our ancestors were still earthlings, hobbled by biology and doomed to return to dust. Perhaps. Sci-fi literature is filled with stories like that. Biological life may be just a stage in the evolution of postbiological life.

Nowhere to Run

It is actually somewhat worse than Lyotard lets on. Lyotard never mentions the larger inescapability of cosmic disaster, the final entropic dissipation brought on by the accelerating expansion of the universe not only of our solar system but of every solar system, of everything. (Or, if not that, then the Big Crunch, which will be equally devastating to our universe.) There is nowhere to run from the fact that everything is running away from everything else. So the question of hope arises from two givens: first, that like it or not we are inherently futural beings, turned toward the future, full of hopes and fears; and, secondly, the relentless expansion of universe, the doomsday destiny described by the cosmologists. Do the math. *Pace* Epicurus, we cannot simply switch that knowledge off. We cannot dial it down to zero and conclude that taking into account the final fate of the universe is idle curiosity.

Does hope have a future? In what can we hope?

Is technology the Sabbath of life? Don't count on it. It is an opening onto the future fraught with risk and uncertainty, shot through with anxiety about an unforeseeable to-come. Far from supplying us with a day of rest, it requires around-the-clock watchfulness about what we are doing with our bodies and our future. Its promise contains a threat; its hope harbors a fear.

Was Yahweh right after all? Right to station a guard around the tree of life? Was this just petty jealousy about his own immortality? Or was he onto something, that it is not mortality but immortality that is ruinous? Are there grounds for hope, even biblical grounds, in the seemingly inescapable fate of our mortality? Is the best thing for mortals to remain mortals? Is life a struggle against death in which the struggle is the victory, even if death has the final word? Is that the message of the deathless stars, which we know nowadays are no more deathless than are we?

How is any of this of any help—to Jackie or Brother Paul or anybody else?

CHAPTER EIGHT

Do We All Die? Everyone? Life before Death

Years ago, I remember watching "The Waltons" with the older of my two sons, who was seven years old at the time. It was the episode portraying the death of Grandpa Zebulon Tyler, which had been written into the script when Will Geer, the actor, actually had died.

"Dad, does everyone die?" my son asked me.

His question threw me into a panic. I wanted to disappear into thin air, even though, in a way, this was my field of specialization!

"Yes," I said, appearing calm. But he followed up.

"Everyone?" I could feel his reply rising from a disbelief that an abyss so immense and inescapable could be so commonplace. My God, was there no way out of this question, no way to escape from this room?

"Yes," I said, still keeping my composure, but knowing that his life was about to change.

I did not say I have spent my life staring into this abyss, that when he heard me upstairs typing in my study (no word processors yet), that is what I was writing about. I have never written about anything else than death, God and death, whatever the difference between those two spectral companions may turn out to be, if there is any difference at all.

■ ■ ■

So what now? That is what Jackie wants to know, and Brother Paul. So do I.

Now I come to my point, or rather now I must face the music. I grew up in a world where I was taught that divine omnipotence supported the promise of living forever, just so long as I did my part—which mostly meant that I did not anger the priests and nuns who taught me this valuable lesson, did not miss Mass on Sundays and holydays of obligation, that I kept my hands off the girl next door and, most important of all, did not become a Protestant. I would later on conclude that this version of religion, which has been given ample time to prove itself, has spun itself out. The philosopher that emerged in me would come to greet that story with a measure of incredulity. It is implicated in a basic mistake about what is going on in the name of God.

The question now, put very simply, is, what now? If we square off with nihilism, if we face up to the facelessness of the inhuman, of implacable death—divested of the God of Omnipotence, who makes our enemies our footstool, disarmed of the Lord of Hosts and of the gods of technology, and armed only with a rose—what now? What good is this alternate religion of the rose when it comes to cosmic nihilism? Is there any hope for hope, any hope in religion, even one of a very different sort that is never going to win approval in Nashville or the Vatican? What good is such a religion to Jackie and Brother Paul, to the other Jackie and to our sister Marguerite, to Hegel and Lyotard?

What now?

Life before Death: Eschatology in a New Key

The dream of techno-immortality cannot head off the inevitable irreversible end of everything in entropic dissipation and thermal equilibrium. Nor is it headed off by the head-in-the-sand-ism of Epicurus. There is no escaping the *eschaton*, the ultimacy of death—personal, planetary, solar, cosmic. But the question is, Are we asking the wrong question? Is escaping death really the issue? Does death, the prospect of death, spell the death of hope? Is it eternal life—or nothing, *nada, nihil,* nihilism? Or is that a kind of blackmail that has kept a certain kind of religion in business for far too long?

In another time and place I might have told my son that life is defined by the finality of death, but it is not nullified. Is a painting nullified because it has a frame, or a playing field because it has foul lines? Such limits do not destroy these things; on the contrary, they make them possible. Looked at in a larger long-term biological way, death is regenerative; it is the way the torch of life is passed on to a new generation and life is renewed. That's another way of saying it's the only way to get some people to retire.

Looked at from our own more short-term and personal point of view, the thought of death, however difficult a prospect to contemplate, in fact promotes the intensification of life. The intensification arises not from the actuality of death, of course, but from the prospect; not from being actually dead but from our being exposed to death at every moment of life. As an actuality, our own death is an unthinkable paradox, since every time we try to think it, we find we always manage to survive, to remain around to do the thinking. How can we think the unthinkable? But then again, how can we *not*? So it is the prospect of death, the foreseeing of what we cannot see coming, which is our inescapable spectral companion. I am always thinking this unthinkable thought, day and night, Jackie and I and Brother Paul, all of us. It is enabling, not disabling. For nothing stretches our faculties further, nothing intensifies our life more, than trying to think the thought of the unthinkable, to represent the unrepresentable, to go where we cannot go, to do the impossible.

Nothing does—*nothing* does.

But do not dismiss this nothing too quickly. Do not treat it as nothing at all. This nothing is creative, not just for the species but for us, for me, for Jackie, Brother Paul, the professor, the husband, the father and grandfather, that make up this corporation which, in a vast oversimplification, in a highly dubious shorthand, I call myself. Here we encounter a *creatio ex nihilo* that has nothing to do with omnipotence theology (which was, by the way, created almost from nothing back in a second-century theological debate and is not to be found in the Scriptures). This is *creatio ex nihilo* in a new key, tuned not to the Why in the Sky of classical eschatology, but to the creative forces that issue from the contact between being and nothing, from the sparks given off upon reaching the border between life and death. There, on that border, life is intensified to its limit.

When someone is in an accident, hovering between life and death, even if—especially if—we do not like this person, we are brought up short, struck dumb by the solemnity of the situation.[1] A passage to the limit like that raises life to a fever pitch, pushing thinkers and artists and relief workers to the limit of their capabilities. Being toward our end ontologically *before* reaching it chronologically—the very prospect of death that Epicurus tried to suppress—carries us like rushing waters up against the ultimate, washes us up against the *eschaton*, and gives rise to a new and unnerving eschatology. Here Heaven is replaced with the heavens, the fires of hell are doused in a cold dark expanse, and the focus of classical eschatology on life after death is replaced with a new focus on life before death.

The "before" in life-before-death means both anterior to, as in the life we are given before we die, and standing before death, as in being brought before a judge. Here every day is "Judgment Day." We stand before death as before a cold black expanse that lets the light of our little life stand out like a star in a blue-black night. Against the backdrop of nothing, being stands disclosed.[2] The passage to the limits is not destructive but creative, not dispiriting but inspiring, intensifying the vitality of mortality in our *vita mortalis*. It is only when we press against these limits that hope and faith are quickened. I do not mean a hope and faith that have been confined by a confessional creed and condensed into formulas used to beat death at its own game, to mock its victory. I have grown weary of the long robes speaking with authority in matters in which we are all non-knowers. Their false security cuts off the creative mystery of our lives, subjugating life to its Why, reducing religion to magic.

The passage to the limits leads to a more exposed, unprotected, and abysmal faith, a more uncertain hope against hope, a *credo* menaced from within by incredulity. Everything that I have been saying up to now depends upon emancipating faith and hope from the police, releasing them from the menacing grip of both Religion and Pure Reason, and letting them tremble like reeds in the wind, in all their precious and precarious fragility. Let faith and hope be like the birds of the air, like the lilies of the field, like a rose that blossoms unseen in a remote corner of the universe on a little piece of matter circling a star whose light we see now but was extinguished millions of years ago.

To think the unthinkable is to attempt to make contact with something unconditional under the concrete conditions of the real world. That of course is impossible, but we take a strange joy in the impossible, in trying to sound the mystery of our lives. We seek to plumb depths we cannot reach, to touch a bottom with which we can resonate but not reason. If I ever dared to write a book on Pure Reason I would argue that the faculty of reason refers to the power to resonate with depths we cannot fathom, while "pure" means unprotected. The inhuman, that terrible night in which death itself has died, where nothing is "left behind," also belongs to an uncanny joy that marks the human. The creative power of living before death depends upon exposing ourselves to the end, life reaching out and touching with its fingertips the finality that gives it definition, like Michelangelo's Adam and God at the moment of creation. The scene of the inhuman sparks the imagination of science and art, of philosophy and theology. It sets us musing over the end-times and ignites the great compassion of mortals for their fellow mortals, constituting a community of mortals, all siblings of the same dark night.

In What Can We Hope?

Given the prospect of the inhuman, of a cosmic nihilism, what hope is there for hope? How to hope against hope? Why are we all so fascinated by a cosmic catastrophe? How is hope ignited by extinction instead of being extinguished?

Do we all die? Everyone?

Religion, if it is worth its salt, is peppered with hope. What we call religion in modernity, along with its antecedents in antiquity, and its analogues outside the reach of Greco-Latin-European languages, is a name for the endlessly different ways that human beings meditate their mortality and craft a hope for something that eludes our ability to come up with names. In naming it the unconditional, as we do here, we are simply using shorthand, explaining that we will never cease to seek and to find new ways to name it. We are always seeking a way to speak without speaking of what we speak of as unspeakable. This failure is a permanent feature, not a temporary one we can repair later on, because in speaking of hope we are trying to come up with a name for the coming of what we cannot see coming.

Everything turns on the temporality of our lives and the incredulity it induces about eternity. The ancients said time is a moving image of eternity. I maintain that eternity is a mistake we make about time. It is not a pure intellectual mistake, or an error in calculation that a computer error check could ferret out. It is a more deeply visceral fear of the transiency of time, of the fact that every time we say "now" things have changed and now it is no longer (the same) now. Now cannot be maintained, taken in hand (*maintenant*), held in check. Our personal time is running out and there is nowhere to run. That is why the Epicurean solution to death is a sheer rationalism, which might have convinced Mr. Spock, which means you have to be half Vulcan to be persuaded by it. But is almost amusing to counsel beings who live in time and can feel time rushing through their bodies to stop thinking about the future.

Lyotard knew it but did not quite say it. He taunted those of us who, however skeptical we may otherwise be, continue to believe in something, in anything, be it philosophy or art, theology or ecology, private life or political life, wealth or power or pleasure. "You're really believers," he said, "you believe much too much in that smile." By the "smile on the surface of matter in a remote corner of the universe," he means what the philosophers call the "life world," the world we live in, spaceship Earth, this little bit of blue in the black expanse, where stars race away from one another at an accelerating pace, headed straight for oblivion. Plato, looking up at stars that had died eons ago, declared them deathless. But against the measure of this "inhuman," even the "atheists" are believers; anybody who believes anything, who fights for anything, is a believer. The interminable debates between theists and atheists, the unanswerable questions of the philosophers, the clash of political ideologies, the upheavals in the history of science, art, and politics—these are all lovers' quarrels, intramural disputes raging among earthlings off in a corner of the cosmos. These debates are all contained within the larger community of "believers," like a political argument raging in the bar on the *Titanic* just minutes before it hits the iceberg. They all end up in the cold black icy drink of the deep.

Seen from a distant point in outer space, they *all* believe in the smile, and they argue only about its finer points. Is it broad or subtle? Can it take different forms? Does it always mean the same thing? Does the smile have a first cause or a teleological purpose? Is it bound by laws or is it a random bit of chance? Is this a divine smile or just an anonymous formation, like a canyon carved out of rock by flowing water? Even those who are mean and miserable enough to be concerned only with themselves, everyone else be damned, still believe in something and think that life has a meaning, however narrow, narcissistic, and self-centered, however inhospitable and ungiving and unforgiving that meaning might be. They may be mean as a hornet but they are not in despair. Furthermore, even those who allow themselves to languish in utter despair, utterly devoid of even a trace of hope, caring no more for themselves than for others, even they, though they have lost their hope in the smile, confirm it *privatively*. They suffer from being deprived of the smile and their suffering bears witness to it in a negative mode, the way a parched earth bears privative testimony to the water it so badly needs. Even Lyotard's darkest musings on his darkest day are one more case of the smile, one more deep and teasing exercise of attempting to think the unthought, to represent the unrepresentable, to name the unnamable. As any writer can tell, Lyotard is obviously having a good time.

As healthy eighteen-year-olds, we once asked the Director of Novices when temptations against the vow of celibacy would subside, to which he replied "about fifteen minutes after you're dead." Funny, but also a good answer, and true here as well, with faith and hope. The only real nonbelievers, the only ones to really give up hope, are the dead. We stop believing in the smile, hoping against hope, about fifteen minutes after we're dead. The only ones without religion, the passion of another religion lacking ecclesiastical approval, are the dead.

Lyotard is using the word *believers* where I prefer to speak of faith and hope. Lyotard is boiling away the differences among the particular beliefs that people might have and boiling them all down to being "believers" in the smile, no matter how divergent these beliefs may be and how mightily they might clash. As a terminological matter, I have distinguished the multiplicity of particular beliefs from an underlying "faith." Henri Bergson called this faith and hope our vital force (*élan vital*), which is a good point because in modernity the word *faith* has come to suggest something more intellectualistic and less carnal than what I am getting at, which belongs to a more elemental, affective, bodily mode of being in the world. A belief (*doxa*) expresses a "position" and it comes accompanied by supporting propositions, like buttresses that keep orthodoxy's cathedrals from tipping over. Orthodoxy is uprightness, which is alright on a flat earth, but in a global world it means we are all pointing in a different direction.

Lyotard was taunting the philosophers for loving unanswerable questions—even as we have taunted the theologians in the Little Church who love unquestionable answers! The part that really interests me is the unanswerability, the endless, irrepressible flow of self-interrogating life. That bears testimony to the *driving force* of the questions, the *élan*, the underlying faith and hope, which along with love are the very stuff of religion, a certain proto-religion, the only use for the otherwise extremely troublesome word "religion." What I am getting at *sub rosa*, under the name of the rose, of the religion of the rose, is a certain uncertain religion, whereas "beliefs" are more like movable furniture. Life is more like jogging than driving to work; the joy is in the journeying, not getting to the terminal destination! This faith and hope emerge as a fidelity to the world, a bodily affective feeling-for-the-world. Heidegger spoke of our "attunement" to things, the way our body is tuned to the world, to the earth and to one another, which he said sets in before and beneath the cognitive chatter going on up above. This faith is what the body professes long before the professors arrive at the scene, notebook in hand, ready to describe what happened. That is why Nietzsche called the body the big reason and the mind the little reason. This faith and hope are the fundamental momentum of our being-in-the-world, a faith and hope in the future, a faith in the promise of the world, which dares to hope in the future as well as in the past, and can come about under many names and many different forms of life. Life is the smile that breaks out on the surface of matter, and faith and hope return that smile.

If you lose your faith in the sense I mean, you have lost your faith in life; you cannot go on. The joy has gone out of your life. If you lose your hope in the sense that I am exploring, life collapses in a heap upon itself, the light dims down to a pinpoint and then disappears. The smile is gone. Everything stops. Martha walks off the job. The petals fall from the rose. You have lost faith and you no longer dare to hope.

Daring to hope, hoping against hope, having hope in the smile on the surface of matter, having the audacity to return that smile against the dark skies of personal, social, global, solar, or cosmic death—the anatomy of that smile, the dynamics of the faith and hope that respond to that smile, the ups and downs of that smile, its promises and its threats—that is the subject matter of the religion I here defend under the name of the mysticism of the rose.

What we call the "humanities"—the very things that are increasingly at risk in our means-ends, cost-accounting world, where the universities are being gradually turned over to the MBAs—are *ex professo* the effort to trace the lines of the smile, to track its lines of force. The humanities are the marks left on hearts wounded by the inbreaking of the unconditional. They are at bottom very mystical undertakings, which is why they have trouble getting funded in the economy of the university, where they are expected to turn a profit.

I have my whole life been constantly exploring this religion, like a blind man feeling with a stick, refocusing the discussion upon matters of a more elemental faith and hope. I fear they will be held hostage by the police of religion, become the subject of creedal wars, of the worst bloodshed, one more alibi for murder. I am interested in what lays claim to us unconditionally without force or pageantry, without the huffing and the puffing, without the adornments and the armaments of "religion" (or the State or the Party or Reason). I am in pursuit of something that religion contains without being able to contain, a religionless religion far too important to leave to "men" of "religion," who earn a profitable living off our anxiety. I am interested not in coming up with another proof for the immortality of the soul or the existence of a super-being in the sky, but in matters of the heart, in saving the word *religion* from religion.

CHAPTER NINE

A Short Catechism on the Nihilism of Grace

The meaning of life came packaged and delivered to Jackie in no uncertain terms in a catechism, a series of questions the answers to which Jackie learned "by heart." The nuns made sure of that—or else! So it is fitting to reciprocate and to bring this all to a head by means of a kind of counter-catechism. In this little catechetical Q and A, an advocate of a more traditional religion, of a mind much like the one found in Jackie's catechism, puts questions to my new species of theologian, who answers on behalf of the nihilism of grace. The answers given here I fear would have been beaten out of him by Jackie's nuns—although they might be graded more favorably by the nuns of today. His nuns would have none of today's nuns, who are pretty nearly the last voices of dissent and of unintimidated resistance in the Church, unless of course Pope Francis succeeds in doing the impossible and creates a Church that is not in headlong flight from science and the contemporary world, which is our hope against hope.

■ ■ ■

Q. Why do you keep calling your taste for the mystics religion? What is so religious about it? You want to keep a safe distance from the Bible-thumping and the billboards attacking the theory of evolution, I can see that. But what is left over is an odd duck and it seems to me disingenuous to call it religion. Wouldn't it be more honest to say you no longer believe in religion and set the whole idea out in different terms?

A. To be precise, I call it a religion with or without religion, or a proto-religion, which I think is the sort of religion that most merits our faith. But this is not a concoction of mine, something I just made up. I have taken it from the mystics, who I think of as my informers, my contacts on the inside. This religion does not break in upon religion from the outside but irrupts from within religion. I am not forcing anything on religion, or doing anything to it. I lack the wherewithal for that. Religion itself already contains something that it cannot contain. Religion of itself is already inwardly disturbed and made restless by itself. Whatever we call it, a rose by any other name would blossom without why.[1]

Q. But where's the religion?

A. Religion begins and ends with grace. All that matters to me is that we treat life as a grace.

Q. But is not grace given by God?

A. To be sure, grace is given in and under the name of God. When a grace happens, it brings the name of God to our lips. But of itself, a grace is a happening, a gratuity, a gift, something that did not have to happen but did. We are here today and gone tomorrow as Jesus says of the lilies of the field, earthly reeds blowing in the cosmic wind. Our fleeting existence is a passing moment on the cosmic stage, a grace we are granted for the while, for which our life is lived as a prayer of unthinking gratitude.

Q. But to what or to whom?

A. To something-I-know-not-what, something that did not ask to be thanked and had no intention of being gracious. Life is a gift we did not ask for. That is the condition of a pure gift, of an unconditional gift—no Infinite Debt, no Big Benefactor in the sky, no choirs of courtiers singing eternal hosannas to the emperor, no rewards and punishments. Just a gift, without why. Take it. It's yours. Enjoy. The enjoyment is all the gratitude there is. No one knows anyone gave anyone else anything. Grace is God disappearing into the world from sheer love of the world.

Q. But grace is given by God as a means to attain our salvation. What purpose does grace serve for you?

A. What purpose? If someone gives you a gift, are you so ungracious as to ask its purpose? The pure gift is given without why and received without debt. That's the whole idea of the gift, and that is the very idea of grace. Grace is grace only if it is given *gratis*. If there is "why" attached to the gift, then whatever that is, it is not a gift. It has something up its sleeve. It is masquerading as a gift, presenting itself as a present. If a gift comes with strings attached, if it has a why and a wherefore, then it is not a gift we are dealing with. It is just a deal, incurring a debt that will come due later on when the creditors show up at our door. The gift is for free, given for nothing. A grace has a special good-for-nothingness about it where the nothingness preserves the purity of the gift. That is what I call the nihilism of grace.

Q. Then just what do you mean by nihilism?

A. Nihilism is the cultivation of nothing (*nihil*). It comes in many forms and it is risky business, like a fire that can either warm a house on a winter night or burn the whole place down. Nihilism is edgy business, living on the edge of being, on the slash between being and nothing. It is a source of despair *and* a source of hope, not one without the other, and so it should not be dealt with lightly. The turn I give it here is to turn the water of cosmic nihilism into the wine of the nihilism of grace. The nihilism of grace is hidden in plain sight. It sits silently in the center of cosmic nihilism, waiting to be noticed, according to the logic of being-*for*-nothing, living life without why. The nothing is the purifying fire of the gift, which burns off every why and wherefore.

Q. But I don't understand. What is life for? What are we living for?

A. Life is not *for* anything else. What would that something else be if it were not more life? "If a man asked life for a thousand years, '*Why* do you live?' if it could answer it would only say, 'I live because I live.' That is because life lives from its own ground, and gushes forth from its own. Therefore it lives without *Why*, because it lives for itself."[2] There is nothing for which you could exchange life even—and *especially*—if we give up our life for another. For then we do so for the *life* of the other. To give life to the children is to give to a future we will not live to see. That is the greatest gift possible, as Jesus said, the perfect expenditure without return (John 15:13).

Q. People can make the Scriptures say almost anything they want.

A. Well, that's because the Scriptures say almost anything you want.

Q. All this seems to me to say, with a certain razzle-dazzle and postmodern mumbo-jumbo, is that ultimately everything serves no purpose. Doesn't nihilism mean that life is full of sound and fury and signifies nothing?

A. When Lyotard poses the problem of the inhuman, he gets as far as the "purposelessness" and then seems to stop. What he takes as an objection to life is rather a clue to its real point. Purposelessness is not a problem but the very condition of grace, of the gift of grace, which comes without benefactor or debt. Life is not a coupon you turn in for a reward at the end. It is not an admissions ticket for a trip to another world. Life is not trying to reach its "end."

Q. Don't you see what you're saying? If it is purposeless, it is meaningless.

A. It is without a purpose, not because it falls short of a purpose, like an obsolete tool that no longer serves a use, but because it is in excess of a purpose. It is not less than purposeful but more than useful. It is without a purpose in the sense that it cannot be treated as means to some long-term and external end; it does not *serve* a purpose like that. A particular thing in the world may be of service to another, but the world as a whole is not in service. To treat the world like that is like someone who would buy a Picasso in order to cover a stain on the wall. But nonetheless it is, as Kant said of the work of art, purposive without having any purpose. It has a strictly internal meaning, its own internal quality, delight, and form, without serving as a means to a further end. It is like an Arabesque where the lines have meaningful internal relations to one another without leading out to something else which they represent.

Q. Stop trying to be so confusing. Yes or no, does life have a meaning?

A. There is a meaning *in* life but not *of* life. Life is not subordinated to a meaning. Meanings, in the plural, along with a lot of other things, musing, feeling, loving, are all ingredients *in* life.

Q. Even so, all well and good, but this is only for a little while. Is it not fleeting and transient and perishable and will not last forever?

A. Precisely.

Q. Do we not all die?

A. Yes.

Q. Everyone?

A. Yes.

Q. If that's all there is, we live for a while and then we're dead and gone, doesn't that ruin everything?

A. On the contrary, that is why life is so precious. The fact that things do not last forever does not undermine their value; it constitutes their value. If life lacked this temporality, it would lack value. Nothing would be at risk, and so nothing could be promised. Nothing could be lost and so nothing could be gained. Nothing would be threatened, so nothing could be hoped for. Meaning and value would suffocate at the oppressive presence of what is always safe and can never be lost. The world would be a solid ball of presence, without spaces and gaps, without differentiation and articulation, rhythms, moments high and low, without room to breathe.

Q. But is not eternal life the highest and the best, the greatest good?

A. That is to confuse the unconditional with the eternal. That is the perpetual illusion perpetrated in Platonic-Augustinian eternalism, to which even my beloved mystics fall prey. Lacking the respiration of time's passing we would expire before our time, simply give up the ghost and without quite dying live on as un-dead. It is mortality that gives life vitality; immortality is lethal. The fruit of the tree of life is poisonous. Immortality is the really forbidden fruit. That life takes a fleeting and evanescent form does not demolish its meaning; it defines it.

Q. Wouldn't life be a waste of time?

A. The mistake is to think that time is wasted unless it is put into gainful service as a means to gain eternal rewards. It is an illusion to think that a thing has to last forever to be worthy of unconditional love, that it has to reward us with eternal life, otherwise we are wasting our time on it. That I consider the real laying waste to time. That is a failure of nerve, a lack of faith in life, a breakdown in hope. What is first and last is not the eternal but the unconditional, what is affirmed for itself, not for its ability to last forever.

Q. But maybe the unconditional is eternal. Why not?

A. The eternal is what cannot not be. But the condition of the unconditional is the risk that it just might not be, that it will not happen. The eternal is necessary; the unconditional is exposed to the "perhaps." So not only may the unconditional not be eternal, it cannot be eternal. There cannot be a promise unless there is a threat. There cannot be a good unless it is menaced by evil. There cannot be a real journey unless we are good and lost. This is the point that Lyotard leaves out—it is precisely our mortality that makes our life unconditionally precious, the inhuman that makes us cling to life so tenaciously, like lovers in the night who know they must part in the morning.

Q. And you call that religion?

A. On my reading, the ultimate "religious" gesture lies in the affirmation of the unconditional, and the unconditional requires a double and symmetric risk. First, the risk that God takes to disappear into the world without remainder, into the rose blossoming unseen and for a while, off in a distant corner of the universe. Secondly, the corresponding risk on our part is to live like that rose, to affirm life unconditionally, without the expectation of a reward or the fear of a punishment.

Q. How can such a thing even be imagined?

A. Imagine a science fiction movie whose title is "Lost Planet." The film is all about a distant planet, off in a galaxy far, far away, where life slowly and laboriously evolved until it reached a point of flourishing and magnificence. In this film there were beings there who experienced some counterpart to what we call love and enmity, joy and sorrow, heroism and cowardice, wisdom and folly, art and science, beauty and ugliness. As the film progresses, the universe moves on and the little planet has to die. It orbited around a sun whose light we only see now but the sun itself exploded many millions of years ago. It disappeared forever, totally unknown to us or to anyone else. We know nothing of them, or they of us, and nothing is remembered, no one is there to remember. Would you say then that all that life on the lost planet was in vain? Did its transiency undermine its worth? Does it make all that life futile? Is there any sense to ask what purpose that life served? Is it not enough that it happened, that it came to be, flourished for a while, and then passed away? For a while it was true that there was truth, life, a world, that a rose blossomed because it blossomed. Finally, at the end of the film, we discover this distant planet is an allegory of our life on Earth, a post-Copernican update of Plato's geocentric allegory of the cave and the sun.

Q. I still don't see why you call this religion. Isn't religion supposed to save us from all that?

A. Then forget religion, or cross it out, or put an asterisk (which means a star) beside it. Religion,* religion-with-an-asterisk, is a way to name the smile and to celebrate it as a grace. By religion I mean a way to hail the glory of the smile, to magnify the glory of the rose, a way to hail a world full of grace. It is a way to affirm the grace of life, of all life, not just ours, and to affirm the world, living and nonliving, every world, not just our little corner of this universe. Its ultimate virtues are faith and hope and love of the smile. Its ultimate prayer is to say yes to the promise of the world, amen to life in all its mortality and contingency, "come" to the event of the world, to time and its becoming, yes to what we cannot see coming. Yes, yes, amen, come. While keeping our fingers crossed that life is not going to be a disaster (a lost star).

Q. Is that not a religion only a philosopher could dream up?

A. On the contrary, we can find it anywhere. On my accounting, God, religion, and theology can be found anywhere. This life of religious affirmation is lived, this amen rings out, this "come" is called, this yes is affirmed in many ways—in a work of art or of philosophy or the dazzling adventures of science, in a life dedicated to the service of others, in a private life or a public one. It is found in a famous celebrated life or an obscure life unknown to the world. It is found in great world-transforming deeds and in tiny fleeting moments of quotidian life. It is celebrated when we feel a sudden breeze on our face, or the bracing bite of cold, in moments of exhilarating exertion or sheer exhaustion, when we sink like lead into bed at night, in those tiny crevices of daily life in which life itself breaks out, breaks through, breaks in, like Proust's cup of tea and a madeleine. All of these forms of life or ways to be, all these passing moments—all the things that make us what Lyotard calls "believers"—will have been religious. In that sense, we are all religious and a certain faith and hope in life make us what we are. That is what is going on *in* religion, its most audacious moment, with or without, inside or outside, the various religions, in all their countless varieties, known and unknown.

Q. You keep talking about hope, but if all this ends in entropy, in what can we hope?

A. The life of hope is hope in life itself.

Q. Then forget religion, forget God, and just talk about life. Why do you keep on talking about God?

A. This is not me talking. This is talk that had already started without me. That is why I myself cannot *not* talk about God. God will not go away, not because God is a necessary being but because God is contingent, a part of the world I have inherited. Were I born elsewhere, at another time, all this might be different, something else might be going on. The name of God is a paradigmatic name for me and there is nothing I can do about it. All my life I have heard these voices whispering in my ear, from my earliest memories as a child. It is a paradigmatic name for me, for a lot of "us," meaning for those of "us" who find themselves situated in one of the cultures of the great monotheisms. But I do not take the name of God to be the name of a being, of an existent, but of a way I have been overtaken by the world.

Q. I am confused. Are you saying that the name of God is a way to describe the world or that the world is a way to describe God?

A. That is a lovely undecidability. Is the rose a pseudonym for "God" or is "God" a pseudonym for the rose? This undecidability is irreducible and this irreducibility gives life its salt, its depth and resonance. Kierkegaard insisted on the need for the pseudonymity of the religious author, in order to protect the privacy of the individual's one-to-one relationship to God, lest a *tertium quid*, a mortal third man, intrude himself in between them. I propose a further step, the pseudonymity of God, God as a pseudonymous author of the world, lest the overbearing omnipotence of the creator crush the flower blossoming unseen in some remote corner of matter. Such omnipotence would replace the smile we return to the world with a look of craven fear before eternal flames or a look of spiritual greed for eternal life outside the world. The blossoming of the rose without why—is that the highest praise we can give to "God"? Or is "God" the highest praise we can give to the rose, to the smile on the face of the world? I love this undecidability and am nourished daily by it.

Q. Your nihilism embraces the cosmic destruction, but what if the scientists change their mind?

A. Entropic dissipation is the dominant view of the scientists at the moment. I certainly am in no position to contest the results of their work. I maintain a subscription to *Scientific*

American and I am happy if I can just follow what they are saying in the table of contents. This is what they are saying now and that may change. Some physicists say that the present universe is but one universe in an endless series of universes, each universe spawning another, so instead of a linear trajectory we have a continuous recycling, an endless repetition, without beginning and without end, *literally* world without end, amen![3] That would give Gertrude Stein's line "A rose is a rose is a rose" still one more gloss. Whether or not the end of our universe is the beginning of another, let the chips of science fall where they may. I find no cause for despair in physics.

Q. Why not?

A. Lyotard's idea was to look for some way around the end of thought. My idea is to follow the end of thought to the thought of the end, to look the eschaton in the eye, to see in this purposelessness, this blossoming without why, the very audacity of God to disappear into the smile of the world, the very world that the physicists tell us is itself disappearing, if not quite before our eyes at least before the mathematical eyes of the astrophysicists. The traces of that smile are inscribed in the appearing of what is disappearing. The smile is etched out on the surface of matter in motion. Beyond being a thing *in* the world, the rose is a figure *of* the world. The world as a whole is the rose that blossoms for a while, and then disappears. We are that smile, our life is that rose, and we celebrate it. When we turn to God (*à Dieu*), as if to escape from worldly tumult into the Sabbath of life, God dares deflect our look and turn us back to the tumultuous promise of the world.[4] God bids us adieu: to turn to God is to return to the smile of the world.

Q. So do you think that the world is God?

A. No. There is a version of that idea that tempts me, but I resist it. The name of God is the name of something unconditional that is going on *in* the world, of some spark *in* the world to which we respond with the vocabularies of poetry and religion. So I preserve a creative distance between the insistence of God and the existence of the world. God is the name of an event that interrupts the world and brings it up short, of something unconditional without force. This as opposed both to pantheism and to the fearsome visage of a testosterone-rich Zeus-like patriarchal superhero called God, the Father, the Why in the Sky, which I think has been laid to rest by what I like to call Yeshua the earthman.[5] The name of God is the name of a grace, which is but a passing moment in the life of the universe, a moment of faith and hope and love, so that God like the rose is mortal, fleeting, and transient. God is as mortal as anything else.

Q. And so the dignity of humans is to be the privileged bearers of the smile?

A. Not quite. Do not other things smile? Meadows and animals? We have had too much of such humanisms, and it has nearly killed us and a lot of other, nonhuman species. All things, human and nonhuman, are on this account compatriots, companions, siblings of the same dark night, bound together on this point of common perishability. All creatures great and small have their religion. All pay common homage to the whole and express our common religious natures by coming to be for the while, "whiling," in the verbal sense, not merely whiling away but glowing white hot for a while, for a micro-moment in the history of the universe, and then returning to the inexhaustible from whence we came. We greet the cosmic smile on matter with a smile of our own, exchanging greetings for that passing moment in cosmic time when we meet—and all too soon have to part. Maybe it has happened many times over again throughout the cosmos that a little bit of stardust eventually grew arms and legs and a head and began to argue with itself about the existence of God. Perhaps.

Q. With this much interest in modern science, are you going back to the Enlightenment after all?

A. According to the old Enlightenment, which challenged the old pre-Copernican religion, the highest audacity is to dare to think (*sapere aude*). I am all for that, all for thinking, the more the better. But I prefer to think in terms of a new Enlightenment, after the disappearance of God into the world, where the highest audacity is to dare to hope. I think that thinking is daring but hope is even more daring. Dare to hope in the smile, in the rose of the world, in the spark of life that is given us as a gift for which we did not ask. Dare to hope in a gift that gets itself given without a generous donor and without a debt to repay. That is the much riskier gift of the nihilism of grace. A gift without an Almighty All-Generous Omni-Giver taking all the credit, hogging the stage of this fragile, precious, and delicate scene of gifting. It means being gifted by gifts without a giver, being gifted without why. The grace of life is granted us for a given time, for a fleeting moment of cosmic time, our birth being an answer to a call we never heard, an amen to a prayer uttered before we were born.

Q. Prayer? It never stops. Where did that come from? In a religion without religion, where God does not exist, how—in God's name, if I may say so—would we pray? To whom? And why?

A. I was saving that for last, as a kind of closing prayer, as my recessional.

CHAPTER TEN

Conclusion: Dreaming, Praying, Hoping, Smiling

One of Jackie's favorite nuns was named Sister Rosa Mystica. A lot of the older nuns were tough, but she was young and pretty, a gentle heart and kind to the children. But still, Jackie thought, of all the odd names taken by the nuns from the long litany of saints of whom he had never heard, this is one of the odder, and he smiled secretly to himself about it. Jackie had no idea, of course, that the mystical rose would save his life.

It could not have occurred to him that it would be the stuff of a lifelong search, the subject of a recurrent dream, a matter of constant prayer and meditation.

It all started with a memory, unless it was a dream, a secret strictly kept between Jackie and me, about whether the paltry presence of our little species is simply overwhelmed by the immense sprawl of stars above. It continued with the meditations of Brother Paul, a serious young man who had decided to engage the economy the Church offered: a life of a teacher, which he would certainly love, he was sure of that, and of prayer and daily Mass and communion, a formula he firmly believed would store up treasures that would never rust. A wise rustproof, mothproof choice, over which, only later on, would a certain incredulity settle like an early-morning fog moving in over a large sleeping city. The dream continues to this day, a voice whispering in the ear of a professor professing to know something about such things, or at least mastering the art of pretense. The whole time, at every point along the way, all of us, Jackie, Brother Paul, and the professor have been praying; dreaming and praying; hoping, dreaming and praying; smiling, hoping, dreaming and praying— of what? Something, we know not what. But the non-knowing is not a defect, like a leg missing from a table. It is the very core of the knowing, where what we manage to know is like water rushing from an unknown source, where there is always some recess still unknown, still coming, still calling.

Dreaming

I confess the whole thing is a dream—and in an effort to save a few dollars I interpret my own dreams.

A dream that gives me no rest. Night after night, tossing and turning, the same dream, the same restlessness, and in the morning I wake up with a start. I am dreaming of a pure gift, a pure expenditure without return, which would be a nightmare to the accountants. My reverie leaves me fearful over its fragility—how might something that fragile be capable of moving mountains? Not to mention the nightmare—how fearful it would be were a thing of such seductive and delicate charm to be seized by the authorities! Cheapened by an economy of exchange, immured within institutional walls, calcified in a creed, made murderous with blood and sword, used to supply an ancient alibi for murder!

I am dreaming of what the gift would look like were it free. Were it not bound over to people who pose as authorities in matters in which we are all novices and non-knowers; were it not contracted into dogmas by people writing under the pseudonym of God; were it not distorted by the twin pathologies of inerrant books or infallible institutions, of popes real or paper. I am dreaming of a gift not policed by the self-appointed professionals, by those whom Kierkegaard mocked for trying to earn a profitable living off the Crucifixion. I am dreaming of a word that would name a unique variety of human practices dedicated to the cultivation of gifts and of all things that exist without why, of all things great and small that sway under the gentle breeze of the unconditional, that have been touched by its sweet breath.

I am imagining a certain form of life for which we lack a more felicitous name than religion and a structure within which it may reside commodiously and without violence. I readily concede upon waking that in the real world what I am dreaming is impossible. *The* impossible. That is why life without a why is a dream. But instead of having the sense to give up, my madness is that the impossible drives me on, asking me to give it one more go. Trying to go where it is impossible to go—that is what is going on in what I have sometimes called my religion.

I am trying to interpret my own dreams. Maybe I would do better if I paid a shrink to help me with this, but that would require I spend money I do not have. Sometimes I awake in the middle of the night, a little boy in the dark, whether awake or still asleep I am not sure, wondering what is going on. Whither and whence these voices in the dark? Was that a dream at all or some spooky presence right here in my room? Is it the world that calls? Or God? Or what my beloved mystics call the "soul"? Or my guardian angels, whom the nuns assured me would be always by my side? Or nothing more than a piece of undigested beef?—which is Dr. Nietzsche's diagnosis of the psychology of the religious soul, about which they never told me in Catholic school.

I am dreaming of what the other Jackie calls the unconditional, something that lays claims to me unconditionally, but without force. It is this lack of force that angers the powers-that-be, who fear nothing more than being without power. I dream of sneaking into their camp under the cover of night and cutting off their power supply. Their Super Being, a force of fantastic proportions, who is going to save us. Their Super Judge who is coming to settle the hash of the world at the End of Time. Their Big Truth, along with their police, who are supposed to enforce it and pacify everything. Their idolatry. Their God. What they call, in a sustained and ancient mystification, in which is concentrated an ancient history of violence, God. Their conflation of the gift with what they dare call God. Their confusion of what is calling and being called for in and under the nameless name of something unconditional, with a Super Hero they call God. Their confusion of their God with the mystery sometimes known as God.

I am visited nightly by obscure nocturnal spirits in the small hours of the morning, specters who inspire a meditation on subtle and elusive matters. They dissipate in the daylight hours, their soft sighing drowned out by the boisterous verbal bombast, the thoughtless diurnal debates, the tiresome wars waged between the antagonists of this and that, of religion and secularism, of faith and reason, theism and atheism. I wait patiently for night to fall again when my spirits will reassemble, telling tall tales of a long-lost land where they take care to cultivate everything that exists without why.

The play of the gift cannot be contracted into a logic, even a theo-logic. It requires instead the lighter touch of a poetics, or of a theopoetics, a soft song to the most elemental conditions of our lives. It longs for a lyric way to give words to something stirring beneath and within the propositions and entities that take up our wakeful daytime hours. Propositional truth is diurnal, while nocturnal truth is more meditative.

The song soars up to the heavens and there dissipates into the clouds. It bears witness not to an immaterial soul that will live forever but to something of a carnal kind, deeply mortal. The song sings of a life inscribed in corruptible flesh and bones, deposited in the depths of corporeal being. It makes no bones about our mortality, which cuts deeply into our hides and hearts, like nails driven into our hands and feet. The beauty of the song, like the beauty of the rose, depends upon the rhythms of mortality, the pulsations of alternating joys and sorrows, the heights of comedy and the depths of tragedy. It sings of lives inscribed in the earthiness of space and etched by the waters of time, forged by the fires of pain and held upright by the winds of joy. The song sings of living things, things that are born, that flourish for a while in the bloom of youth, and finally have to die. Then I awaken with a start. Was there someone in this room? Someone singing?

I am dreaming of what is to-come, of a gift to-come, of a God to-come. But do not think I am dreaming of escaping to another world where I will finally be safe from the difficulties and struggles of this one. The reality and the severity of the world, of Martha's world, the structures, institutions, and traditions, the demand for reasons and causes, cannot be simply brushed aside with the wave of a poetic wand. Nothing is simple. Without the structures of human culture, nothing would be cultivated, accumulated, and passed down. Without the Church, of which I have been known sometimes to complain, there would be no memory of Jesus and I would have nothing to dream about. The ancient texts and memories would have simply scattered to the four winds. Dreaming of what is coming is never a question of dismissing the structures of culture but of cultivating them, keeping them open to the future, ready and able to reinvent and reproduce themselves. My dreams do not inhabit another world but spring up in the crevices and interstices of this world, like so many marks of punctuation of the world. We live in the distance between dreaming and actuality, between Mary and Martha, between the poetry and the prose of the world, between the unconditional and the conditional. To live without why is to find a caesura, a pause, a moment of silence, in the ceaseless rush of why's and wherefore's. We live with/out why, both with and without, neither with nor without.

I am not dreaming of doing away with religion. I am trying to save religion, not only from its critics but from itself. I am trying to recover something that is going on *in* religion, something that religion "harbors," meaning both keeps safe and conceals. Religion hovers over the abyss of the gift and it is afraid to look down. If you are suspended over an abyss and what suspends you is without why, if your grounds are groundless, don't look down. Just go where you cannot go.

I hear whispers in the night, voices barely audible, and when I awake I take up a pen and pad I keep on my nightstand and try to get it all down before it slips away. Something about God, about love, about something coming, just what, I cannot make out.

In the daylight hours I cling as tightly as I can to the figures, tropes, traditions, and texts I have inherited. I am not trying to humiliate and demean them as primitive superstition. I do not say they are pure superstition. I say they are spooked, which for me is a salutary thing. Where there are spooks, there is hope. To be spooked is to be haunted by the spectral coming of something we cannot see coming, which means to have a future, and futures require hope. So I try to savor the Scriptures, to rock in unison with their songs—all in order to release their uncontainable excess, some dream I think which hovers over or maybe inhabits the Scriptures from within. I am dreaming of the way that finite things are pried open by the infinite, dreaming of the infinitival promise of what is "to-come," which should not be confused with eternal rest, which is how we describe cemeteries. My spooks whisper aspirations in my ear. They have nothing to do with cemeteries. I am not ready for eternal rest; even when I sleep, my sleep is restless with the coming of something I cannot see coming.[1]

My money-saving effort to interpret my own dreams takes the form of a hermeneutics of the gift. The key to my self-interpretation is to treat the rose as a figure of grace, of the sheer gratuity of life without why, the gift of grace, the grace of the gift. I am dreaming of a way to emancipate grace from the grip of the powers-that-be, to let it flourish in a free city beyond the jurisdiction of the authorities, the Big Men of both Religion and Reason who try to bully and blackmail us in our diurnal life.

I dream of finding a place for grace, a room in a crowded city that is neither the city of God nor the City of Man—in both places there are cameras on every corner—but a city of refuge. Only there can grace flourish, beyond the surveillance of the police of truth, who seek to regulate and domesticate its unnerving fortuitousness and unforeseeability; who seek to incarcerate those they deem mad; to excommunicate the dissidents; and to silence those who would speak volumes of the unsayable silence of the abyss of grace, of the gift that is given without why.

Praying

It would require many books to describe the indescribable depths of life without why. So it is fitting that I leave you with a prayer, a little recessional, as Jackie, Brother Paul, and the professor, and all their friends and correspondents, gather up their things and head for the door. We have spent our whole life, all our waking hours, just as the Apostle says (1 Thess. 5:16-18), always praying, praying like mad, praying like hell! My first, last, and constant prayer is "Come," which is the penultimate word, which almost has the last word in the New Testament

(Rev. 22:20), almost its final adieu, its bottom line, its punch line, its prayer.

I have earned calluses on my knees trying to learn how to pray, trying to lead a life of prayer, or to follow one, to be led in prayer by something, I know not what. Prayer is passed off as the private property of the pious. That makes me laugh. They do not know that the other Jackie (Derrida), impudent and impious and atheistic as he was, was a very prayerful man. But the pious have to make a buck, and conducting prayer services is the main way the clergy pay their bills. Their union is not going to let these jobs get out of their control without a fight. They would shut the churches down before letting that happen. The idea of the prayers and tears of the other slightly atheistic Jackie, or of Eckhart praying God to rid us of God, or of praying without the long robes leading the prayer, all this leaves them red in the face and crying unfair labor practices. If someone consents to *lead us* in prayer, what else can that be than the blind leading the blind? Blindness is the human condition over which, from which, in which we pray. I only object when it is the blind who do not know they are blind leading the blind who do! We cannot lead a prayer; we can only follow it into the unknown.

Nonetheless, I admit that the long robes have a point. I admit that, seen on the surface of the inhuman landscape portrayed by Lyotard, the sort of prayer I am describing seems to be a nullity. I see why they see nothing more than nugatory supplications sent up to an indifferent sky, sighs destined to dissipate into a stellar night, praying without a why or a wherefore. Can such prayers as these be anything more than voices drifting off into a void, the last vanishing traces of the smile on the surface of matter? Anything more than songs sent up in a universe that does not know we are here? Soft sighs drowned out by spectacular solar explosions and noisy comets zooming hither and yon? So many roses withering away in a cold dark expanse?

Perhaps that is all they are. But that would not be an objection to prayer; it would be all the more reason to pray. In the sanctuaries of the pious, to pray is to pray to "someone," to ask for this or to give thanks for that, and to have a good reason to think there is someone there to answer and handle the correspondence. Compare that to the notion advanced in the religion of the rose that the name of God is not somebody's proper name, a Big Somebody with the power to deliver the goods, the power to be the giver of all good gifts and to make our enemies our footstools! Well, I admit it. Such prayer is a shaky enterprise. It promises no payoff. It is a stumbling block and foolishness!

I pray, night and day, that someday some devilish knight of faith will come along and make my dreams come true. I am dreaming of the appearance of some rogue of a fellow who will be the answer to my prayers, precisely the sort of chap the powers-that-be in religion would not take seriously. I pray that he will write a religious masterpiece, a counterpart to Augustine's *Confessions*, one of the magisterial works of "religious literature," if ever there were one.[2] I do not underestimate the difficulty of such a thing. We say the *Confessions* is the West's first great autobiography, and that is not entirely wrong. But the genre of the *Confessions* is more strictly considered a prayer addressed to God in writing, which we readers are invited to overhear. So the entirely unauthorized author of this heretical counterpart to the *Confessions* in this religionless religion will have his hands full. He will have to be a bit impish and impious to pull this off, unafraid of posing stumbling blocks and of appearing foolish. He will also have to have the devil in his eyes. I pray for the coming of a devilish fellow who would evoke from us Kierkegaard's line about finally meeting an actual knight of faith: Good Lord, is this the man? He looks like a tax-collector.[3] He will have to come up with a prayer that begins by making the open confession that we do not know how to pray, or to whom we are praying, or whether there is anyone to answer our prayers, or what we are praying for.

The pious no doubt will mock the whole thing. How is it possible, they will protest, to pray to an unknown God, to pray without knowing if anyone is there to hear our prayer? But how, this rogue will reply, the devil in his eye, is it possible *not* to? How *not* to pray precisely when we have been left without a prayer? Especially since this non-knowing has always and already been found *inside* prayer, inside the prayers of the mystics, in the dark nights of the soul, in moments when the only thing of which these men and women of prayer are sure is that they do not believe in prayer or God or religion. The tradition is full of warnings about the danger of knowing too much when it comes to prayer, which is why the ancient masters tell us to be careful what we pray for, on the grounds that we may get it. The masters realized that when it comes to prayer, there are no masters of the house, that while we consciously desire this or that, we do not know what we desire with a desire beyond desire, and that this non-knowing, which makes prayer impossible, is just what keeps it possible.

Prayer begins by openly confessing the constraints that make prayer impossible, while quickly adding that in a religionless religion that is not an objection. Such an impossibility is the only condition under which prayer—or any other matter of elemental

importance, like faith or hope or love, hospitality or forgiveness—
is possible. If prayer or anything else were simply and straight-
forwardly possible, we should engage in it only under protest. If
things were simple, if we knew what we were doing and how to
do it, where we were going and how to get there, to whom we
were praying and how what we think we desire could be realized, we should want nothing to do with it. In a genuine prayer,
one that is something more than a bit of bourgeois propriety, or a
way to get elected to public office, we are hanging on by a prayer,
left without a prayer, utterly unable to pray. I have been praying
all my life. I have worn through the knees of several pairs of very
good pants. But if you persist in asking me to whom, or to what,
I am praying, I would plead with you, I would pray you, please,
be reasonable. If I knew that I would know everything. I would
be omniscient, fused or confused with God. I would be entirely
relieved of my precariousness—which is, I would add, where we
get the very word prayer (from the Latin *precari*)—and hence in
no need of prayer. The only thing that makes prayer possible is
that it is impossible.

Wrested free from the grip of the palace theologians,
released into the never-never land of the gift, we can say that to
pray is to expose ourselves to risk, to roll the dice, hoping against
hope, hoping for a chance for grace, which is dicey business.
Prayer is not for the risk-averse. I am praying, weeping, dreaming, under the name of the rose which blossoms because it blossoms, dreaming of twisting free from all the omniscience and
omnipotence that suffocates prayer and extinguishes the chance
for grace. I am trying to shelter a secret something that no omniscience can see coming, trying to cultivate a contingency that no
omnipotence can miraculously make happen. I am praying for

the coming of what is promised in words of elementary promise, for events stirring obscurely in promissory notes, words like justice, friendship, hospitality, gift, forgiveness, and democracy—and so forth—where the devil is in the details.

"And so forth," aye, there's the rub. Perhaps my devilish knight of faith would also find time to publish a book on this inscrutable, almost infinite "and so forth," which would contain a lexicon of all the possible names that could be added to this list. Seeing that the unconditional, which is my candidate for what is going on in the name of God, can happen under any conditions—inside religion or outside, in art or science, on mountaintops or in city streets, in moments of high drama or in quotidian life, in the chambers of the powerful or in ghettoes—where would it all end? Would such a list of what we are praying for ever end? As Eckhart says, in saying God is unnameable we are also saying God is omni-nameable, which is why the mystics say so much about the unsayable—and say it so eloquently, I should add. My publishers would panic at the cost of such a book. Perhaps it would have to be an e-book that would enkindle our hearts, a bit of heavenly cloud computing that would hold down the cost. (Far be it from me to ignore questions of economy!)

In the language of this religionless religion I have been practicing all my life, over which Jackie and Brother Paul and the professor have held countless nocturnal consultations, toward which I began to drift at some not quite identifiable moment after I took up the philosophical life "*ex professo*," I would now say that we pray for what *insists* in these words. It is this insistent spectral spirit that haunted Jackie and Brother Paul and brought them to their knees, which ought to bring us all to our knees, which is not to say that we cannot pray standing up or while taking a brisk walk or driving home from work. Whatever our position, profession, or posture, prone or peripatetic, to pray means to risk exposure to some spectral something or other, something unconditional but without force. To pray is to acknowledge that something calls upon us to bring these promises to fruition, to fill up what is lacking in these wispy spirit-like bodies whispering in our ear or disturbing our sleep, reminding us that it is our business to supply existence to their solicitous insistence.

To pray is to keep the world restless with the future, where the God of the gaps means the gaps God opens, not the gaps God fills. To pray is to be prompted by the promise of the uncompromisable, moved by the memory of the immemorial, pushed beyond the limits of the possible by the impossible. Prayer prevents the present from closing in upon itself and from closing in all around us. It keeps the world in a state of optimal disequilibrium, exposing the world to God's pressing insistence. Prayer is a way to keep faith with life, to sustain the hope that the future is always better, to better pledge our love of the unconditional. Prayer tends to the shoots of justice struggling to grow in the cracks of the parched surfaces of the world. Prayer does not commune with the eternal but exposes itself to the disjointedness of time. The time is always out of joint. Time itself is being out of joint. That is why we pray.

Lord, lead us not into the temptation to betray the world, to sell out the world for thirty pieces of religious silver. To pray is to cling resolutely, rigorously, religiously (using the alternate etymology), to the purity of the gift, to an element of the rose that blossoms because it blossoms. Prayer does not demand a deal to make prayer worthwhile. Prayer does not subordinate the promise of the world to the promise of another world, behind the scenes, above and beyond the world. The world is a gift, not leverage in a deal with a Supreme Being who holds all the cards.

So to the scandal of the Religious Man, the subjects of the City of God, and as a bit of foolishness to the Man of Reason, the citizens of the City of Man, I say, let us pray. *Oremus*. Let us dare to pray. *Precari aude*. Let us dare imagine prayer differently, dare rethink where it happens, dare widen our idea of who is and who is not leading a life of prayer, daring to pray outside the sanctuaries of the pious. A prayer is a wounded word, a sigh sent up by a wounded heart.[4] What deeper wound, what heart more restless, than one deprived of the classical assurances of an omniscient, omnipotent omni-answer to all our prayers? One of the most poignant images in the Scriptures in this regard is Jesus going out into the desert to pray, accompanied only by his animals (Mark 1:13). The desert is a figure of solitude, but also of aridity, of conditions under which only the hardiest desert flower can flourish. That is why, in traditional prayer, we are advised to begin a prayer by praying even to be able to pray. When we say, Lord teach us how to pray, Lord hear our prayers, we are already praying while being unable to pray! Praying to be able to pray is the first, last, and constant prayer, the prayer we pray always and everywhere.

Hoping

Finally—or rather, first of all, because this is how I started—whether waking or sleeping, I am always hoping. The rose on my coat of arms is the figure of hope, of hope against hope, hope in the face even (and especially) of the facelessness Lyotard describes so well. In the religionless religion of the rose, hope is one of God's virtues, too, as we learn from an old Talmudic story in which the rabbis say that God tried but failed to create the world twenty-six times before he finally succeeded. "'Let us hope it works' (*Halway Sheyaamod*) exclaimed God as he created the world, and this hope, which has accompanied the subsequent history of the world and mankind, has emphasized right from the outset that this history is branded with the mark of radical uncertainty."[5] God too is dreaming. God too is hanging on by a prayer. God too is hoping against hope. We are in this thing together, we and God, and we cannot let each other down. What thing is that? The thing of the world. The thing of it is the world. Hope means that things are neither steered mightily unto good by an invisible wisdom nor hollowed out at their center by some primordial catastrophe and doomed to fail. Hope means that things are just unstable, risky, nascent, natal, betokening neither an absolute plenum nor an absolute void. Smiles can be wiped away; laughter can turn to tears. Hope means that the world contains an uncontainable promise, which is also a threat. Hope means that a great "perhaps" hovers over the world, that what holds sway over the world is not the Almighty but a might-be. But "perhaps" does not signify an attitude of lassitude or indifference. "Perhaps" is risky business, a resolute staying open to a future that is otherwise considered closed. "Perhaps" continues a discussion that the authorities considered closed. "Perhaps" is not indecisive but is fueled by the audacity to hope.

The world stirs uneasily under the undecidable fluctuations of the promise, trembles under the tremors of the "perhaps," rises and falls with the tides of expectation. Religion, the religion of the rose, not the religion that tries to keep itself safe at any cost and to promise salvation, but one more audaciously conceived, is the record of these pulsations, embracing the exhilaration of the promise/threat. Hope is the risky business of calling for the coming of what we cannot see coming, of saying yes to the future, where nothing is guaranteed.

I honor the audacity of the old Enlightenment, dare to think, *sapere aude*, but I love a second audacity even more, dare to hope, *sperare aude*, by which the first is haunted. Hope hovers over us like a ghost, whispering in our ears impossible things, waking us with a start in the night. Hope is a spirit, the aspiration, the very respiration of God's spirit, of God's insistence, which groans to exist. Hope dares to say "come," dares to pray "come," to what it cannot see coming. Hope is hope in the promise of the world, inscribed on the surface of matter in a distant corner of the universe, in a rose that blossoms unseen, blossoming because it blossoms, without why.

Smiling

At the end of life, just as in the beginning and the middle, the only thing to do is to say thanks be to life for life, for the grace of life.

Thanks be to the stars for their loving anonymity. The anonymity of the stars is a sign not of their indifference, as Jackie and Brother Paul feared, but of the depths of their mysterious love. We are not to blame them for not knowing that we are here. We should instead thank them for the purity of their gift, for not trying to be omni-generous benefactors or to put us in their everlasting debt. Even their everlastingness is a bit of a show; it is not quite what it is cracked up to be.

I have a dream in which young Jackie meets the other Jackie, who shows up one day as a long-lost uncle. How an Italian Catholic family could have an Algerian Jewish slightly atheistic uncle fortunately requires no explanation in a dream. In the evening on the porch, looking up together at a starry sky, Uncle Jackie mentions to the youngster that he has a recurrent dream about the stars. Just then I awake, sure I heard voices in the room. I do not get to hear the rest of the conversation, but I am sure the two of them hit it off.

At the end of his life, the other Jackie, my candidate for a devilish knight of faith, left us a little message:

> Smile at me . . . as I will have smiled at you until the
>   end.
> Always prefer life and never stop affirming survival.
> I love you and I am smiling at you from wherever I am.[6]

The End

Off in a distant corner of the universe, unknown to the stars around it, a little spark is ignited and a light is born. The light grows steadily larger and stronger until finally, in a great burst of energy, it flares up and flares out, extinguished without a trace, its little life and gentle smile unknown to all its neighbors. The light burns because it burns, in all its brilliance, and then the little star has to die and the universe moves on.

Amen.

Alleluia.

Oremus, says an aging priest in Italian American Latin.

Notes

CHAPTER ONE

1. Cited by Benoit Peeters, *Derrida: A Biography*, trans. Andrew Brown (Malden, MA: Polity, 2013), 541.

2. As will become clear below, *A Game of Jacks* is a fiction of my own devising.

3. *Hoping against Hope* is an exercise in what the French call *haute vulgarisation*, a slightly highbrow popularization, of what I have to say to a strictly academic audience in *The Weakness of God: A Theology of the Event* (Bloomington: Indiana University Press, 2006), which was awarded the 2007 American Academy of Religion Book Award for Excellence in Studies in Religion, "Constructive-Reflective Studies"; and *The Insistence of God: A Theology of Perhaps* (Bloomington: Indiana University Press, 2013). For readers with a taste for more theoretical and technical accounts, I will supply a few key references to the academic literature in the footnotes.

4. The first one I came across, and there is none better, is from the youthful Nietzsche in "On the Truth and Lies in the Nonmoral Sense," in *Philosophy and Truth: Selections from Nietzsche's Notebooks of the Early 1870s*, ed. and trans. Daniel Breazeale (Atlantic Highlands, NJ: Humanities Press, 1979), 79.

5. Jean-François Lyotard, *The Inhuman: Reflections on Time*, trans. Geoffrey Bennington and Rachel Bowlby (Stanford: Stanford University Press, 1991), 8–12. This is presented as the perspective of the "He," which is followed by the perspective of the "She," to whose cause I am rallying in this little book. I first discussed this text and Nietzsche's in the first chapter of my *Against Ethics: Contributions to a Poetics of Obligation with Constant Reference to Deconstruction* (Bloomington: Indiana University Press, 1993). For Lyotard's famous definition of postmodernism, see Jean-François Lyotard, *The Postmodern Condition: A Report on Knowledge*, trans. Geoff Bennington and Brian Massumi (Minneapolis: University of Minnesota Press, 1984), xxiii–xxiv.

6. Lyotard, *The Inhuman*, 10–11.

7. Jacques Lacan, *The Triumph of Religion Preceded by Discourse to the Catholics*, trans. Bruce Fink (Malden, MA: Polity, 2013), 63–65. Lacan, of course, is being sarcastic.

8. I will examine the provocative analogy between this theological solution and Lyotard's technological solution (escape from the limits of the body) in chapter 7.

9. The phrase is adopted from Herman Melville's *Bartleby the Scrivener*.

10. See Immanuel Kant, "What Is Enlightenment?," accessed August 23, 2014, at http://www.columbia.edu/acis/ets/CCREAD/etscc/kant.html.

11. For a brilliant portrait of such Catholicism by someone who is almost my exact contemporary, see James Carroll, *Practicing Catholic* (Boston: Mariner, 2009).

12. Richard Dawkins, *The God Delusion* (New York: Mariner/Houghton Mifflin, 2008).

13. I am acutely conscious of the patriarchy of theology and when I say "men," or speak of God as a male, I am doing so intentionally, with "incredulity," and in a critical spirit, like the "He" of Lyotard in *The Inhuman*. For the most part, the God of religion and the people of this God have been conceived in aggressively phallocentric terms and on this point I follow the lead of the feminist theologians who have been getting in the face of patriarchy for many years now.

14. Jacques Derrida, "Circumfession: Fifty-nine Periods and Periphrases," in Geoffrey Bennington and Jacques Derrida, *Jacques Derrida* (Chicago: University of Chicago Press, 1993). I will come back to this book several times, including in my final prayer (ch. 10), as it is a touchstone piece for me.

15. Dietrich Bonhoeffer, *Letters and Papers from Prison*, ed. Eberhard Bethge, trans. Reginald Fuller, Frank Clarke, et al. (London: SCM, 1971), 278–82.

16. The heart of my strategy in *The Insistence of God* is to have recourse to this expression, "what is going on" in the name of God. This is worked out by means of what is called the middle voice in Greek grammar, which is something in between an agent doing things and a recipient receiving them. I do not regard God as an agent who does things, but that is not the end of God, since things get themselves said and done in and under the name of God.

CHAPTER TWO

1. See Foucault's discussion of Jean-Baptiste de la Salle, the founder of the Brothers of the Christian Schools, in *Discipline and Punish: The Birth of the Prison*, trans. Alan Sheridan (New York: Vintage, 1977), 177–84.

2. Thomas Merton, *A Vow of Conversation: Journals 1964-65* (New York: Farrar, Straus & Giroux, 1988), 59. My thanks to Patrick Cousins for pointing out this text to me.

3. *The Mystical Element in Heidegger's Thought* (Athens, Ohio: Ohio University Press, 1978; revised paperback edition with a new "Introduction," New York: Fordham University Press, 1986).

4. Angelus Silesius, *The Cherubinic Wanderer*, trans. Maria Shrady (New York: Paulist, 1986), 54. See Meister Eckhart's articulation of the mystical logic of the "without" in *The Complete Mystical Works of Meister Eckhart*, trans. and ed. Maurice O'C. Walshe (New York: Crossroad, 2009), 110 ("*In hoc apparuit caritas dei in nobis*").

5. Archibald MacLeish, "Ars Poetica," accessed August 2014, http://www.poetryfoundation.org/poetrymagazine/poem/6371.

6. Martin Heidegger, *The Principle of Reason*, trans. Reginald Lilly (Bloomington: Indiana University Press, 1991), 32–40.

7. In this book I am trying to show that the notion of religious "orthodoxy" is troubled from within. The word comes from the Greek word *doxa*, meaning a belief one holds, the "right" (*orthe*) one. *Doxa* can also mean the beliefs others hold of one, hence one's reputation, repute, or "glory," as in "doxology," which I prefer to orthodoxy. Even "orthodoxy" can be tweaked, as when Peter Rollins suggests "believing in the right way" in his discussion of "heretical orthodoxy." Then orthodoxy starts to inch closer to a doxology. See Peter Rollins, *How (Not) to Speak of God* (London: Paraclete, 2006).

8. See Paul Tillich's brilliant formulation of this matter in *Theology of Culture*, ed. Robert C. Kimball (Oxford: Oxford University Press, 1959), 3–10.

9. François Lyotard, *The Inhuman: Reflections on Time*, trans. Geoffrey Bennington and Rachel Bowlby (Stanford: Stanford University Press, 1991), 10.

10. To smile (Latin: *subridere*, French *sourir*) is a gentler form of laughter (*ridere, rire*).

11. Molly's soliloquy from *Ulysses* can be found at http://poetrydispatch.wordpress.com/2008/06/16/james-joyce-molly-blooms-soliloquy/, accessed August 2014.

CHAPTER THREE

1. See Jacques Derrida, "How to Avoid Speaking: Denials," in *Derrida and Negative Theology*, ed. Howard Coward and Toby Foshay (Albany: State University of New York Press, 1992), 73–142, Derrida's first sustained treatment of the mystical tradition.

2. Marcel Mauss, *The Gift: The Form and Reason for Exchange in Archaic Societies* (London: Routledge, 1990).

3. See Jacques Derrida's treatment of the gift, which has become a central theme in postmodern theory, in *The Gift of Death*, trans. David Wills (Chicago: University of Chicago Press, 1995), chs. 3-4; and *Given Time, I: Counterfeit Money*, trans. Peggy Kamuf (Chicago: University of Chicago Press, 1991), ch. 1.

4. Jacques Derrida and Anne Dufourmantelle, *Of Hospitality*, trans. Rachel Bowlby (Stanford: Stanford University Press, 2000), 83; Jacques Derrida, *On the Name*, ed. Thomas Dutoit (Stanford: Stanford University Press, 1995), 132–37n3.

5. See Bart Ehrman, *Misquoting Jesus: The Story Behind Who Changed the Bible and Why* (San Francisco: HarperOne, 2000).

6. In German, *die Gift* is the word for poison.

7. "Religion is the sigh of the oppressed creature, the heart of a heartless world, and the soul of soulless conditions. It is the opium of the people." Karl Marx, "Introduction" to *A Contribution to the Critique of Hegel's Philosophy of Right*, ed. Joseph O'Malley (Cambridge: Cambridge University Press, 1970), 171.

8. Hans Urs von Balthasar, *Dare We Hope That All Men Be Saved? With a Short Discourse on Hell*, trans. David Kipp and Lothar Krauth (San Francisco: Ignatius, 1988).

9. Thomas J. J. Altizer, "The Revolutionary Vision of William Blake," *Journal of Religious Ethics* 37 (March 2009): 33–38.

10. Even a book intent on protecting this name from idolatry can become an idol. That is why Kierkegaard said that when it comes to our relationship with God, religious authors must learn how to write a book as if they have not written a book, so as not to insert themselves between the reader and God!

11. Mother Teresa, *Come Be My Light*, ed. Brian Kolodiejchuk (New York: Image Doubleday, 2007).

CHAPTER FOUR

1. Marguerite Porete, *The Mirror of Simple Souls*, trans. Ellen L. Babinsky (New York: Paulist, 1993). The "Introduction" (pp. 5–61) Babinsky provides is an excellent entrée to Porete.

2. See Porete, *Mirror of Simple Souls*, 81 (157), 86 (161), 89 (165), 91 (167), 93 (168), 100 (174), 111 (183), 134 (217), 135 (218); I cite by chapter with the pagination in parentheses. For Porete's relationship to Meister Eckhart, see *Meister Eckhart and the Beguine Mystics*, ed. Bernard McGinn (New York: Continuum, 1994), in particular, Maria Lichtmann, "Marguerite Porete and Meister Eckhart: *The Mirror of Simple Souls* Mirrored," 65–86; and Paul Dietrich, "The Wilderness of God in Hadewijch II and Meister Eckhart and His Circle," 31–43.

3. This is explained very nicely by David Kangas, "Dangerous Joy: Marguerite Porete's Good-Bye to the Virtues," *Journal of Religion* 91, no. 3 (2011): 299–319, of which I am making use here.

4. I borrow this excellent expression from Martin Heidegger, *Poetry, Language, Thought,* trans. Albert Hofstadter (New York: Harper & Row, 1971), 1–4.

5. Porete, *Mirror of Simple Souls,* 6 (84)–8 (86).

6. Porete, *Mirror of Simple Souls,* 59 (136). For a commentary, see Babinsky, "Introduction," 27–36.

7. See Amy Hollywood, *The Soul as Virgin Wife: Mechthild of Magdeburg, Marguerite Porete, and Meister Eckhart* (South Bend: University of Notre Dame Press, 1995).

8. *Meister Eckhart: The Essential Sermons, Commentaries, Treatises and Defense,* trans. Edmund Colledge and Bernard McGinn (New York: Paulist, 1981), 177–81.

9. One wonders if Eckhart's interpretation of the story of Mary and Martha was not prompted by reading *The Mirror of Simple Souls,* which we have reason to believe he had seen.

10. See Hollywood, *The Soul as Virgin Wife,* 116–19.

CHAPTER FIVE

1. This is the argument of John Milbank in Slavoj Žižek and John Milbank, *The Monstrosity of Christ: Paradox or Dialectic,* ed. Creston Davis (Cambridge: MIT Press, 2009), 33–43.

2. *Laudato Si: On the Care of Our Common Home.* "Laudato Si" ("Be praised") is a recurrent phrase in the "Canticle of the Sun," composed by St. Francis of Assisi.

3. Apart from the interview with Anne Dufourmantelle, which is more readable, see Derrida's "Hostipitality," in *Acts of Religion,* ed. Gil Anidjar (New York and London: Routledge, 2002), 356–420.

4. See E. P. Sanders, *Jesus and Judaism* (Philadelphia: Fortress Press, 1985).

5. See John D. Caputo, *What Would Jesus Deconstruct? The Good News of Postmodernism for the Church* (Grand Rapids: Baker, 2007).

6. Karl Rahner, "Anonymous Christians," in *Theological Investigations,* vol. 6 (Baltimore: Helicon, 1969), 390–98.

7. Levinas's works are extremely difficult, but I can recommend *Ethics and Infinity: Conversations with Philippe Nemo,* trans. Richard Cohen (Pittsburgh: Duquesne University Press, 1985) as an excellent place to get started.

8. This inherited place may (or may not) be a place of privilege, which goes back to the question of hospitality. It is not enough to say hosts (who

have) should be hospitable (to those who have not). One should go on to ask how it is that one is in the position of a host to begin with? What have you that you have not received? The hospitality we are asked to show the other is a function of the hospitality we have already been shown. The power (*posse*) of the host to offer the stranger (*hostis*) hospitality is not what it takes itself to be.

9. *Kierkegaard's Writings*, VI, *Fear and Trembling* and *Repetition*, trans. and ed. Howard and Edna Hong (Princeton: Princeton University Press, 1983), 200.

10. I work out this argument in John D. Caputo, *Truth: Philosophy in Transit* (London: Penguin, 2013).

11. Jacques Derrida, "Circumfession: Fifty-nine Periods and Periphrases," in Geoffrey Bennington and Jacques Derrida, *Jacques Derrida* (Chicago: University of Chicago Press, 1993), 155. Derrida also discusses his life in *Monolingualism of the Other; or, The Prosthesis of Origin*, trans. Patrick Mensah (Stanford: Stanford University Press, 1998). The biography by Benoit Peeters is invaluable.

CHAPTER SIX

1. *Meister Eckhart: The Essential Sermons, Commentaries, Treatises and Defense*, trans. Edmund Colledge and Bernard McGinn (New York: Paulist, 1981), 200.

2. I make this argument in *Philosophy and Theology* (Nashville: Abingdon, 2006).

3. Rosamond is probably Germanic in origin, from *hros* (horse) and *mund* (protection). But it is deliciously close to the Latin *rosa munda*, "pure rose," and *rosa mundi*, rose of the world, with which it is sometimes happily fused or confused, which is my purpose here, which is not to say that I am not all for protecting horses.

4. To see this developed in more academic terms, see my *The Insistence of God: A Theology of Perhaps* (Bloomington: Indiana University Press, 2013), chs. 1–3.

5. Derrida has worked out the idea of the "unconditional without force" in *Rogues: Two Essays on Reason*, trans. Pascale-Anne Brault and Michael Naas (Stanford: Stanford University Press, 2005).

6. My views spring in part from a postmodern reading of Paul's *kenosis* (Phil. 2:7) by way of Hegel's reading.

7. Heidegger proposed that we say of a particular being or entity that it "is," but of Being we should say "there is" (*es gibt*) Being, since Being is neither a particular being that is nor the sum total of all of them. See "A Letter on Humanism," in *Basic Writings*, ed. David Krell, 2nd ed. (New York: Harper & Row, 1993). The French and German idioms that are

translated into English as "there is" have the advantage that they do not make use of the verb "to be."

8. Paul Tillich, *Theology of Culture* (Oxford: Oxford University Press, 1964), 25.

9. John D. Caputo, "Beyond Aestheticism: Derrida's Responsible Anarchy," *Research in Phenomenology* 18 (1988): 59–73 explains my Eureka moment. The story is incomplete without Emmanuel Levinas, the Jewish philosopher who influenced Derrida and a whole host of philosophers in Europe and North America.

10. If you want to see this worked out in a challenging work of philosophy, see Martin Heidegger, *Being and Time*, trans. John Macquarrie and Edward Robinson (New York: Harper & Row, 1962), §56, pp. 317–19. That's where I learned it.

CHAPTER SEVEN

1. I refer to the work of Aubrey de Grey, a specialist in rejuvenation theory who projects a human lifetime to be measured in centuries.

2. Michel Serres, *Angels: A Modern Myth*, trans. Francis Cowper, ed. Philippa Hurd (Paris: Flammarion, 1995).

3. Jacques Derrida, *The Animal That Therefore I Am*, ed. Marie-Louise Mallet, trans. David Wills (New York: Fordham University Press, 2008), 132.

4. Dale B. Martin, *The Corinthian Body* (New Haven: Yale University Press, 1995), 108–36.

5. Ray Kurzweil, *The Singularity Is Near: When Humans Transcend Biology* (London: Penguin, 2006); Hans Moravec, *Robot: Mere Machine to Transcendent Mind* (London: Oxford University Press, 2000).

6. *The Polkinghorne Reader: Science, Faith, and the Search for Meaning*, ed. T. J. Oord (West Conshohocken, PA: Templeton Press, 2010), ch. 18, "The Resurrection."

7. "A Manifesto for Cyborgs," in *The Haraway Reader*, ed. Donna Haraway (New York and London: Routledge, 2004), 7–45.

8. Shakespeare, *Midsummer Night's Dream*, V, 1.

9. Jean-François Lyotard *The Inhuman: Reflections on Time*, trans. Geoffrey Bennington and Rachel Bowlby (Stanford: Stanford University Press, 1991), 12. He is referring to the work of Hubert Dreyfus.

10. Lev Grossman, "Quantum Leap: Inside the Tangled Quest for the Future of Computing," *Time*, February 17, 2014.

11. John Markoff, "Brainlike Computers, Learning from Experience," *New York Times*, December 29, 2013.

12. See Tom Simonite, "Three Questions for Computing Pioneer Carver Mead," MIT Technology Review, November 13, 2013, accessed August 2014,

http://www.technologyreview.com/news/521501/three-questions-for
-computing-pioneer-carver-mead/.

CHAPTER EIGHT

1. See Charles Dickens, *Our Mutual Friend*, in *The Oxford Illustrated Dickens* (Oxford: Oxford University Press, 1989), 3:443–48.

2. A point made powerfully but in typically enigmatic prose by Martin Heidegger, "What Is Metaphysics?," in *Basic Writings*, ed. David Krell, 2nd ed. (New York: Harper & Row, 1993). When philosophers write like this, it is because they are also praying like mad.

CHAPTER NINE

1. In medieval philosophy, the rose was the standard example in the old debate about names between the nominalists and the Platonists.

2. *The Complete Mystical Works of Meister Eckhart*, trans. and ed. Maurice O'C. Walshe (New York: Crossroad, 2009), 110 (*"In hoc apparuit caritas dei in nobis"*).

3. Paul J. Steinhardt and Neil Turok, *Endless Universe: Beyond the Big Bang—Rewriting Cosmic History* (New York: Broadway, 2007).

4. Emmanuel Levinas makes use of this image of "deflection" in "God and Philosophy," in *Emmanuel Levinas: Basic Philosophical Writings*, ed. Adriaan Peperzak, Simon Critchley, and Robert Bernasconi (Bloomington: Indiana University Press, 1996), 140.

5. See *The Insistence of God: A Theology of Perhaps* (Bloomington: Indiana University Press, 2013), 252–54.

CHAPTER TEN

1. See John D. Caputo, "Proclaiming the Year of the Jubilee: Thoughts on a Spectral Life," in *It Spooks: Living in Response to an Unheard Call*, ed. Erin Schendzielos (Rapid City, SD: Shelter50 Publishing Collective, 2015), 10–47.

2. Since I am putting my cards on the table in this chapter, I have to confess, I think that this book has already been written, by the other Jackie. See Jacques Derrida, "Circumfession: Fifty-nine Periods and Periphrases," in Geoffrey Bennington and Jacques Derrida, *Jacques Derrida* (Chicago: University of Chicago Press, 1993).

3. *Kierkegaard's Writings*, VI, *Fear and Trembling* and *Repetition*, trans. and ed. Howard and Edna Hong (Princeton: Princeton University Press, 1983), 39.

4. Jean-Louis Chrétien, "The Wounded Word: Phenomenology of Prayer," in *Phenomenology and the Theological Turn: The French Debate*, ed. Dominique Janicaud et al. (New York: Fordham University Press, 2000), 147–75.

5. This text is cited by Catherine Keller, *Face of the Deep: A Theology of Becoming* (London: Routledge, 2003), 193–94. Keller herself cites Ilya Prigogine and Isabelle Stengers, *Order Out of Chaos* (Boulder, CO: New Science Library, 1984), 313, whose translation (from the French) we are using.

6. Cited by Benoit Peeters, *Derrida: A Biography*, trans. Andrew Brown (Malden, MA: Polity, 2013), 541.

Index

faith: devilish knight of, 192–93, 195, 200; distinguished from belief, 16, 19–20, 90, 96–102, 131, 160, 164–66, 194; inter-faith dialogue and, 91–96; in life, 177–78. *See* hope; love
Feuerbach, Ludwig, 125
Foucault, Michel, 24
Francis, Pope, 20, 25, 83, 170
Freud, Sigmund, 15
Frost, Robert, 29, 32

gift: creation and, 111–12, 120, 197, 199; distinguished from economy, 34, 34, 39, 47–53, 55–56, 58–59, 61, 68–69, 71–72, 185, 187; economy of salvation and, 64, 66, 104, 110, 184; God and, 61, 120, 192; hospitality and, 84–86, 100, 107, 108; life and, 171–73, 176–78, 182; religion and, 38, 52–53, 58, 109–11,189; time of, 34, 76; works of mercy and, 58–59, 61. *See* Judgment of the Nations; without why
God: guiding idea of, 103–29; letting God be, 30, 131; love and, 60–61, 117, 120–21, 124; needs us, 82, 106, 123–25; religion and, 39, 53, 186; speaking about, 46, 178–79; unconditional and, 107–9, 111, 115–17, 181; weakness of, 105, 124, 128–29; what is going on in name of, 46, 53, 61–62, 82, 107–12, 115, 116, 118–19,121–26, 130, 132, 157, 179, 181, 192, 195, 202n16; will of, 25. *See* death; economy of salvation; gift, insistence; kingdom of God; unconditional
grace: 20, 36, 53, 84, 93; religion and, 35, 40, 171, 177; the world and, 42, 84, 177, 190, 199. *See* nihilism

Haraway, Donna, 146–48
Hegel, Georg F. W., 6, 84, 129, 149–50, 157
Heidegger, Martin: 33, 129, 165; "without why" and, 26–29; thrownness and, 96–97
homosexuality, and welcoming con-gregations, 86–91
hope: death and, 157; the future and, 6, 137, 141, 145–46, 151, 153–54, 196; God and, 114, 120; hoping against hope, 43, 132, 160–67, 170, 194, 197–99; the inhuman and, 6, 136–37, 150, 153–54; nihilism and, 9, 172, 182; religion and, 10–15, 18–19, 157, 177–78; without assurance, 96–106, 117. *See* faith; love
hospitality: conditional vs. uncon-ditional, 85–91, 102, 107; God and, 111, 115, 121; invitation vs. visitation, 88–89; inter-faith dia-logue and, 91–96; Martha and, 84–85. *See* homosexuality

impossible, the, 41, 55, 158, 160, 185–86, 193–94, 196, 199
incredulity: about eternity, 31, 140, 148, 162, 184; Lyotard on, 6–7, 10, 12–13, 15; about religion, 12–13, 15, 16, 17, 19, 36, 140, 157; about special revelation, 95–96. *See* postmodernism
insistence distinguished from exis-tence: the gift and, 58, 108; of God, 61–62, 77–78, 82, 91, 106, 112, 114–22, 123, 125, 127, 129, 181, 196, 199; prayer and, 196
inter-faith dialogue, 91–96. *See* faith

Jesus: the Buddha and, 99; cruci-fixion and, 60; forgiveness and, 41; the gift and, 48, 173; Grand Inquisitor and, 113; kingdom